Care and Repair
of Sails

By the same author

Teach Your Child About Sailing
  (C Arthur Pearson Ltd)

Sails
  (Adlard Coles Ltd)

Racing Dinghy Sails
  (Adlard Coles Ltd)

Crewing for Offshore Racing
  (Adlard Coles Ltd)

Night Intruder
  (David and Charles)

Out in Front – Technical Adviser
  (Sailing film by ICI Fibres)

Jeremy Howard-Williams

Care and Repair
of Sails

Boston, Massachusetts

First published in Great Britain 1976 by Adlard Coles Limited

Copyright © 1976 by Jeremy Howard-Williams

U.S. edition published by
   SAIL BOOKS, INC.
   38 Commercial Wharf
   Boston, Massachusetts

Printed in Great Britain

ISBN 0–914814–06–0

Distributed to bookstores by
   W. W. Norton & Co., Inc.
   500 Fifth Avenue
   New York NY 10036

CERTIFICATE

Thefe Prefents are to certify that

....

a SAILOR OF GOOD REPORT, having begged, borrowed, ftolen or otherwife acquired this booke, and being at all times of SOBER MIEN AND HABIT, is prefumed to have read, marked, learned and inwardly digefted all its teachynges, in particular not to ufe fails in windes too ftrong for ye cloth, not to pull them down by ye leech and in all ways to keep repair ftytches well-fpaced and even, to ye content of him or herfelf.

It being defired to recognife this induftry fo that all citizens fhall know that y^e aforefaid SAILOR has ferved an apprenticefhip of NOT LESS THAN SEVEN DAYS, we declare withal that he or fhe is right worthy to be hight a DO-IT-THYSELF SAILMAKER.

Given under our Articles and Seal

Jeremy Howard-Williams 1976
The Care and Repair of Sails

Acknowledgments

In writing this book I have been lucky enough to have two invaluable sources of advice, widely different in origin. From the vast resources of their Industrial Technical Development laboratories, ICI Fibres have responded most generously to my various enquiries about cleaning sails. Secondly, and no less qualified, my old friend Ernie Vallender, Manager of Ratsey and Lapthorn, has drawn upon forty years as a practising sailmaker to pass comment on my work. To both these authorities I am truly grateful; any errors of fact or fancy which remain are entirely mine.

There is a surprising number of differences between the English and American languages. Bob Mamis of SAIL *Books Inc.* has kindly helped to give the text a mid-Atlantic flavour (flavor?).

Finally, I also have to thank my wife, who once again has typed the words. This is our third book on sails together, and fortunately she has become something of an authority herself, for she has sometimes had to use more than intuition to divine the meaning of my handwriting.

Warsash 1976   JHW

Contents

one
Sailcloth
Construction · Requirements (*Shape Control*; *Modulus of Extensibility*; *Stability*; *Tensile Strength*; *Impermeability*; *Water Absorption*; *Smoothness*; *Chemical Reaction*) · Bias Stretch · Cloth Weight   1

two
Sailmaking
Rounding the Luff and Foot · Tapering the Panels (Broad Seam) · Tension on the Cloth (*Cunningham Hole*; *Headsails*) · Lay of the Panels · Spreading a Sail (*Twine*; *Mainsail*; *Jib*; *Spinnaker*) · Tablings (*Cut Tabling*; *Rolled Tabling*; *Tape Tabling*) · Rubbing Down · Throwing a Tape   6

three
Care of sails in use
Handling (*Chafe*; *Mainsails*; *Jibs*; *Spinnakers*) · Stowing (*Sail Covers*) · Washing · Cleaning (*Wash*; *Adhesive Numbers*; *Blood*; *Mildew*; *Oil, Grease and Wax*; *Metallic Stains*; *Pitch and Tar*; *Paint*; *Varnish*) · Ironing · Winter Storing · Note of Hope   19

four
Examination for Repairs
Mainsails (*Head*; *Luff*; *Tack*; *Foot*; *Clew*; *Leech*; *Bunt of the Sail*) · Headsails (*Head*; *Luff*; *Tack*; *Foot*; *Clew*; *Leech*; *Bunt of the Sail*) · Spinnakers (*Head*; *Clews*; *Leeches*; *Foot*; *Bunt of the Sail*)   31

five
Typical Repairs – Basic Items
Seams · Tablings · Batten Pockets · Patches (*Chafing Piece*) · Spinnakers (*Patches*; *Leeches*; *Chafe*; *Broken Wire*; *Replacing the Wire*; *Broken Tape*) · Roping (*Reroping*; *Casing*; *Tape*) · Headboards (*Chafe at the Head*) · Luff Wires (*Stitching*)   36

six
Repairs to Sail Accessories
Eyes (*Cunningham Hole*; *Reef Points*) · Slides · Hanks or Snap hooks · Windows · Battens · Leechlines (*Leechline Buttons*) · Tell-Tales · Roller Boom Vang · Zippers   48

seven
Examining for Faulty Set
Documentation (*Photographs*; *Notes*) · Tune and Trim (*Mainsail Luff*; *Mainsail Slides*; *Mainsail Clew*; *Battens*; *Main Halyard Tension*; *Jib Sheet Fairlead*; *Jib Luff*; *Jib Sag*; *Jib Hanks or Snap hooks*) · Checks Afloat (*Slack Leech*; *Tight Leech*; *Clew Creases*; *Rope Creases*; *Batten Creases*; *Headboard Creases*; *Sail Too Full*; *Sail Too*

Flat; *Spinnakers*) · Checks Ashore (*Test Rig*; *Leeches*; *Draft*; *Sail Too Small*; *Sail Too Large*; *Cross Measurements*; *IYRU Method*; *Folded Line*; *Specified Points*)　62

eight
Correcting Faults in Set　Tightening Seams · Tightening Tablings · Easing Seams · Easing Tablings · Reducing Mainsail Roach · Pleating · Too Flat (*Moving the Headboard*; *Moving the Tack*; *Headsail*) · Clew Board · Pulling on the Wire · Reducing Spinnaker Fullness · Spinnaker Leech Curl (*Wires*; *Tapes*) · Roping (*Oversewing*)　78

nine
Alterations to Size　Reducing Mainsails · Enlarging Mainsails · Reducing Headsails · Enlarging Headsails · Reducing Spinnakers · Enlarging Spinnakers · Spinnakers of Other Cuts · Altering a Mainsail from Slides to Grooves · Altering a Mainsail from Grooves to Slides　88

Appendix A
Sail Repair Equipment　Needles · Thread (*Hand*; *Machine*) · Beeswax · Sailmaker's Palm · Machine Sewing · Fid or Spike · Splicing Tools · Eyelet Punch and Die · Soldering Iron · Seam Unpicker · Bench Hook · Adhesive Tape · Glue · Leather · Sail Accessories · Sundries　97

Appendix B
Hand Work　Use of the Palm · Hand Twine · Round Stitch · Tabling or Flat Seaming Stitch · Machine Sewing · Roping (*Rope in Tape*; *Taped Luff*; *Hand Roping*) · Darning · Sailmaker's Darn · Sailmaker's Whipping · Repair Tape · Worked Eye · Punched Eyelet · Cringle · A Patch · Splices (*Eye Splice*; *Long Splice*)　105

Appendix C
Altering Sail Sizes　Mainsails (*Shorten Luff and Leech*; *Shorten Luff Only*; *Shorten Luff and Leech*; *Shorten Luff, Leech and Foot*; *Shorten Foot*; *Shorten Luff, Leech and Foot*; *Shorten Foot and Leech*; *Shorten Leech Only*; *Lengthen Luff*) · Headsails (*Shorten Luff Only*; *Shorten Luff and Leech*; *Shorten Luff, Leech and Foot*; *Shorten Foot Only*; *Shorten Leech Only*; *Shorten Leech and Foot*; *Enlarge Headsail*) · Headsail Clew Angle · Flattening Mainsails and Headsails · Making Mainsails and Headsails Fuller · Spinnakers (*Make Narrower*; *Make Shorter*; *Make Wider*; *Make Larger*)　123

one

Sailcloth

Sails are so inextricably linked in all their facets to the material from which they are fashioned, that no book which pretends to examine them in any depth could possibly fail to discuss the way in which sailcloth is made and some of the qualities which it should possess. There is much care and knowledge in the selection by the sailmaker of the cloth he will use for your sail, therefore learn to recognise this wisdom when you see it, for it is part and parcel of his calling. Much will depend on his choice, so let's have a look at some of the points he has to consider.

Construction

Sailcloth is normally woven by arranging threads on the beam of a loom to establish the warp, or lengthwise threads, and then passing the thread back and forth over and under the warp to form what is known as the weft. The resulting weave is tightened by beating up the weft (pushing the cross threads hard up against each other) so that it lies close together, the tighter the weave the higher the cover factor as the weft causes the warp to crimp (fig. 1).

When tension is applied along the warp the lengthwise threads tend to straighten their crimp and open the weft, which makes the cloth more porous and less able to hold any

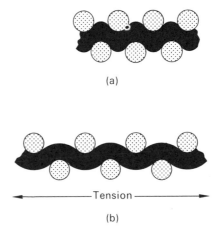

(a)

◄————————Tension————————►

(b)

1. **Crimp**. *The weft of any sailcloth (hatched cross sections) is beaten up together in order to close the weave. This causes the warp (black threads) to undulate in what is known as crimp (a). When tension is applied along the warp, it tends to straighten, thereby reducing crimp and opening the weft (b). This makes the cloth more porous and less able to hold any chemical fillers which may have been added.*

chemical fillers which may have been added; the individual threads may also tend to untwist slightly and thus elongate. But stretch is minimal and no great deformation of the cloth takes place. However, as soon as the tension is at an angle to the threadline (i.e. on the bias) the little squares formed by the weave are pulled out of shape and become little diamonds, so that the cloth distorts by lengthening in the direction of tension and

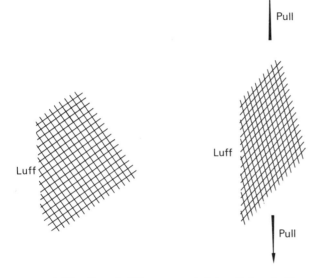

*2. **Bias Stretch**. When woven cloth is pulled on the bias, the little squares of the weave are distorted into diamonds and the cloth contracts across the line of tension. The sail gets no bigger when the luff and foot are stretched – it merely distorts into a different shape.*

narrowing across this line (fig. 2). Cloth therefore moves at right angles towards a line of bias tension, thus forming a fold of extra material along this line; the result in a sail is extra draft along the line of tension and a flattening in the area from which the cloth has been drawn. A good cloth should not

remain permanently distorted after such loadings, but should recover its original shape when the tension is relaxed.

Requirements

The finest cut sails in the world will not last long if they are made of poor cloth. I can best summarise good sailcloth by listing the requirements.

1. *Shape control*. The shape of the cloth should be partly controllable through appropriate tension when trimming sails.

2. *Modulus of extensibility*. This should be high, that is to say that there should be a high resistance to stretch at low loads.

3. *Stability*. It should recover its shape after being subjected to loads.

4. *Tensile strength*. It should absorb energy and stand up to shock loads.

5. *Impermeability*. It should not allow air to pass from one side to the other through the weave.

6. *Water absorption*. It should not absorb water either through a porous weave or into the thread itself.

7. *Smoothness*. A smooth cloth reduces friction drag.

8. *Chemical reaction*. It should not be too quickly degraded by ultraviolet rays, industrial smoke or dirt.

Polyester sailcloth (Terylene, Dacron, Tergal, even Lavsan – its name depends on its country of origin) is virtually immune from the effects of water and from a wide variety of chemicals. It is strong, does not stretch a lot, does not soak up water, and can be woven close enough to be smooth and pretty airtight. The ideal sailcloth, you might say – and you wouldn't be far wrong. However, it can suffer if bits of dirt or salt work their way into the weave and then chafe the threads. In addition, mildew can form around the nucleus of a bit of dirt if damp is present (as it can on glass under similar circumstances). Finally, prolonged sunlight or industrial smoke (constant exposure for a year or so) can weaken the material to the point where it will tear like paper in extreme cases.

A good deal of a sail's effectiveness depends on the way the threads are woven into cloth. As we have seen above, if they are slackly arranged on the loom and not banged up tightly together at each pass of the shuttle, the resulting weave will be loose, porous and stretchy. The aim is for a firm cloth, which is woven under great tension with the weft, or cross threads, banged close together as it builds up on the warp.

Even the highest tension on the most modern looms cannot get the weave tight enough to be acceptable without further treatment. Therefore cloth straight from the loom goes through a finishing stage. During this, it is scoured and dried, may have chemical or resin fillers added to reduce stretch or make the cloth harder, and is then heat-relaxed to shrink and settle the material, thus helping the individual threads to lock together. Resin fillers can give a good initial appearance to a slack cloth, but they tend to make for a hard finish and, if they crack and come out in use, the cloth deteriorates rapidly. The answer for general purposes lies in a tightly woven cloth which needs few chemical additives, thus giving it a soft, pliable finish. Certain fully formed sails for dinghies and the smaller one-design day sailers, on the other hand, do not rely on induced draft for their shape and they get best results from a hard finish, providing precautions are taken to protect the sails from creasing or flogging too much.

Bias Stretch

From the above it will be seen that bias stretch plays a big part in sailmaking. It can be used to draw draft to the correct place, but it can play merry hell with the set and shape of a sail if it is not kept within proper limits. It is the principal reason why leeches are such troublemakers, because they are sometimes not even strengthened by a tabling, let alone a length of rope or tape. If a panel runs at an angle of as little as 5 degrees from right angles to such an unsupported edge, tension down the leech will be marginally off the threadline; this will be enough to cause bias stretching.

Bias stretch is why it is important to see that any patches or reinforcing pieces have their threadlines running parallel to those of the cloth they are being added to, so that they stretch harmoniously. Since cloth stretch varies with the construction of the cloth (the denier of the individual threads which make up the weave, together with the cover factor), the amount of chemical fillers which are added, and the weight of the cloth itself (the heavier cloths are naturally more resistant to stretch), it is also important that any patches are of a cloth as near in weight and construction to the original as possible.

Cloth Weight

In England sailcloth is measured by the number of ounces it weighs to each square yard. In the USA the width of cloth to be measured is fixed at $28\frac{1}{4}$ inches (an Old English standard for broadcloth – ask Robin Hood) and the ounces in every yard of this rather narrower material are weighed; this results in a figure lower by some 20 per cent than in England

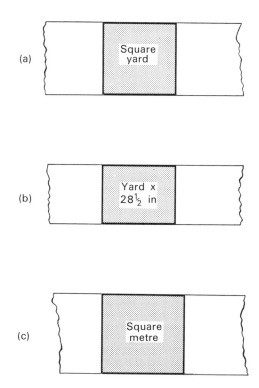

(a)

(b)

(c)

3. **Cloth Weight Measurement.** *Imagine two rolls of identical sailcloth, one of which is 36 inches wide and the other $28\frac{1}{2}$ inches wide. They both weigh the same as each other per square inch, per square foot or per square yard. But the British grade sailcloth by the yard of 36-inch material (a), whereas the Americans weigh the yard of $28\frac{1}{2}$-inch material (b). There is thus more sailcloth to weigh under the British system, which results in an apparent difference, when describing the same cloth, of about 20 per cent. The metric system weighs grammes per square metre (c).*

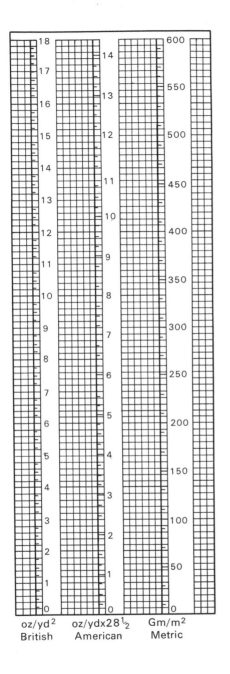

oz/yd^2	oz/ydx28^1/$_2$	Gm/m^2
British	American	Metric

for exactly the same piece of material. When grading a particular cloth, therefore, you have to weigh more actual material under the British system than you do under the American; countries using the metric system weigh the number of grammes per square metre (fig. 3).

A look at the comparative scale (fig. 4) will show that a normal dinghy weight of material for a mainsail and jib of $4\frac{1}{2}$ ounces per square yard (oz/yd^2) in England, is equivalent to just over $3\frac{1}{2}$ ounces per American yard (oz/yd $\times$ 28$\frac{1}{2}$ in) and 150 grammes per square metre (gm/m^2) in the metric system.

4. **Cloth Weight Conversion Table.** *This scale enables comparative weights to be read off at a glance.*

two

Sailmaking

In any study of repairs and faultfinding in sails, it is important to know a bit about how and why a sail is made. If you do not understand what the sailmaker is trying to achieve, and how he has set about it, you will probably do more harm than good as soon as you put a knife or a needle into your sail.

There are four principal ways in which a sail can have draft designed or controlled:

1. Rounding the luff and foot.
2. Tapering the panels (broad seam).
3. Tension on the cloth.
4. Lay of the cloth.

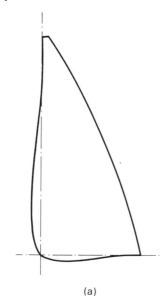

(a)

Rounding the Luff and Foot

If the luff and foot of a mainsail destined for a straight mast and boom are cut in a convex curve, the surplus cloth will be pushed back into the sail as draft when it is put on the spars and the edges are forced into straight lines (fig. 5).

(b)

5. **Luff and Foot Rounds.** *Draft is built into the sail by adding extra cloth to the luff and foot (a). When the sail is set on straight spars, this extra cloth is forced into the sail in the form of fullness (b).*

This draft will lie fairly close to the mast and boom, and the sailmaker will have no control over where it settles unless he adopts other measures as well. There are, however, many successful sails which have their draft arbitrarily designed in only this way. The less round built into the sail, the flatter it will be; little or none will be built in at the head, which may even be slightly hollow if it is desired to keep the sail particularly flat at this point. Sails for bendy spars must have more round, so that they can take up the shape of the spars under maximum curve and still provide the extra cloth required for camber.

A headsail receives similar treatment along its luff. Round is built into the lower half of the sail to provide draft, and it is taken away from the upper half where the sail needs to be flat. In the same way that a mainsail is cut to take up the curve of the mast it will use, so a headsail must be shaped to allow for the curvature of the stay. No forestay can ever be absolutely straight, so the sailmaker must allow for the sag which will occur. Unlike that of the mast, this curve will be towards the rear and to leeward, which will tend to throw cloth into the bunt of the sail and thus make it fuller. The luff must therefore be hollowed to allow for this. The longer the luff the more sag there will be to the stay, so the more allowance must be made (fig. 6).

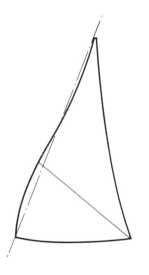

6. **Allowance for Forestay Sag.** *All forestays sag a certain amount, so the luff of a headsail must take this into account. The head should be flatter than the lower half of the sail, so the upper luff is often cut hollow to suit the line of the stay; some fullness should be given to the sail lower down, so we get the curve shown here, where the dotted line represents a theoretically straight forestay.*

Tapering the Panels (Broad Seam)

If some of the panels are tapered, the sail will alter shape accordingly, rather as a dress is

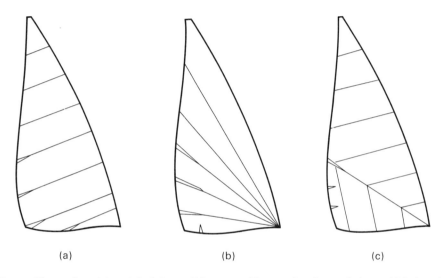

(a)	(b)	(c)

7. **Broad Seam**. *The static position of draft in a sail is governed by tapering the panels from which the sail is made. The horizontal cut (a) lends itself to this treatment but, where seams are not conveniently placed for shaping, special darts may be inserted as in (b) or (c).*

shaped by gussets and gores. If, in addition, the sail has a certain amount of extra cloth built in, in the form of luff and foot round as we have just seen, the position of the resulting draft can be controlled by means of tapering the appropriate panels to a predetermined point.

This tapering of panels is called by a variety of names by different sailmakers, but can generically be termed 'broad seam', and is subdivided into luff seam, tack seam and foot seam. The overall draft given to the sail in the form of luff and foot round will have its point of maximum draft – its powerpoint – along the line where the inner end of the taper ceases.

The horizontal cut for a mainsail is efficient as regards broad seam, because the cloths arrive at the luff at a convenient angle for this purpose. It is for this reason that sails cut in this manner usually have a seam exactly striking the tack, for this is where

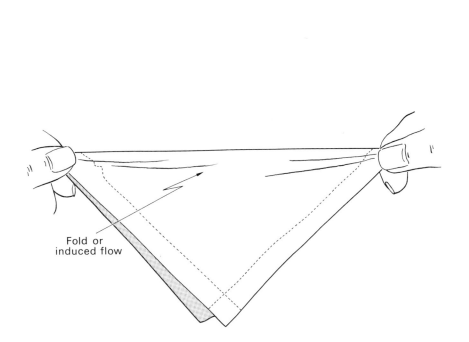

Fold or
induced flow

8. **Demonstration of Induced Draft**. *Fold a handkerchief diagonally and pull the two corners away from each other. This will put tension at 45 degrees to the threadline and will bring a fold of induced draft along the 'luff'; the harder you pull, the deeper will be the fold, and the two loose corners will rise as the 'leech' is drawn towards the 'luff'. Now pull it along one of the edges (i.e. on the threadline) and notice the difference.*

maximum shaping is required. Other cuts, however, must inevitably rely more on darts specially put in for the purpose if no suitable seam presents itself, with the attendant danger of small knuckles appearing where the darts end (fig. 7).

The leech can also be shaped by means of these tapered seams. In this area it is not curvature which is required, but complete flatness to allow the wind to run off cleanly. Thus, leech seams which have been altered at some time in the life of the sail by tightening right out to the tabling should be suspect, because they will tend to hold the leech to windward. Rather should we expect to find these seams eased slightly, particularly near the head and clew, to help free the leech where it has to come up to windward a little to rejoin the top of the mast and the outer end of the boom. Care must be taken not to overdo it, or the whole leech area will go slack and sag to leeward.

Similar broad seam can be put into head-sails, although they need less draft or camber, and can usually be relied upon to take up more naturally their correct shape with the minimum necessary adjustment or darts. A horizontally cut headsail will present plenty of scope for adjustment in this manner.

Tension on the Cloth

We have seen elsewhere that, as cloth stretches on the bias, so it causes a fold to appear near the line of tension. To illustrate this, take a clean handkerchief and fold it corner to corner diagonally in half, so that it forms a triangle. Let the two ends hang down while you pull on the two corners. A fold will appear in the 'luff' of the handkerchief as tension is applied on the bias of the cloth by pulling outwards, and this will deepen as you pull harder. It will also cause the corners hanging down to rise as the 'luff' stretches and the 'leech' is drawn across to supply the extra cloth (fig. 8). Now try pulling straight along the threadline, square with the edge, and notice how much less stretch there is.

When the cloth in a sail is pulled on the bias in the same way, a similar fold will appear along the line of tension. If it is correctly controlled, this tension can be used to induce further draft in a sail. A mainsail is deliberately made shorter on the luff and foot

than its nominal size, so that tension applied by means of the halyard and outhaul will induce draft near the rope or tape. If this tension is applied only lightly, there will be little induced draft, as it is called, and the sail will take up the shape given it by the round and broad seam also built into it. As the wind blows harder, this draft will move aft and up into the sail under the influence of pressure and friction drag. It can be brought back nearer to its starting point again by further tension on the luff and foot.

To be effective, induced draft must be properly controlled. It is no good allowing a sail to be stretched as far as the cloth will go, for this will almost always result in a fold appearing in the adjacent area. First and foremost, allowance must be made by the sailmaker so that a sail does not stretch beyond its marks. Left to itself the cloth would pull out a great deal too much, especially under the influence of powerful halyard winches. However, there is usually a rope or tape on the luff and foot of a mainsail, and this will restrict the distance to which the sail can go. The sailmaker uses a rope with known elasticity, which he first of all pulls to a certain tension before sewing on to the sail. This ensures that there is less rope than sail, thus restricting the amount which the sail can stretch.

Some sailmakers prefer to use prestretched

synthetic rope for the luff and foot of main-sails, particularly for small sails. This has no elasticity at all, and the sail can be cut to its exact shape without having to take account of induced draft through bias stretch. It will still be necessary to pull the sail out to its marks with a certain amount of tension, because the action of sewing the sail to the rope causes a degree of puckering. Alter-natively the rope can be sewn on slack, so that the cloth is pulled a little as the rope straightens under tension.

Cunningham Hole. A Cunningham hole is a means of putting more tension on a mainsail luff which is already out to its racing marks and so cannot be pulled further by its halyard without breaking the rules, as the sail would be stretched beyond the permitted distance. It consists of an eye worked into the luff tabling anything from 6 inches to 2 feet up from the tack, depending on the size of boat, through which a line is passed so that it can pull down on the hole to add tension to the luff when required, thus drawing the sail's draft further forward. Tension on the Cunningham hole will cause a bunch of wrinkles in the tack area, but these are a small price to pay for the benefits gained. Its main use is in light- or medium-weather sails, which can then be made right up to size for their normal use, but where the draft can be

drawn forward again by tension on the Cunningham hole if the wind increases. Equally, a heavy-weather mainsail should always have one, so that the effect of really strong winds pushing the belly right aft can be counteracted by harsh use of the device. It can sometimes give a new lease of life to an old sail where the draft has been blown aft with the passage of time; it is also useful for removing the leech crease caused by bending the mast.

Headsails. When a headsail is made with a conventional luff wire, the sailmaker ensures that the length of the sail luff is slightly shorter than the wire on which it has to be fitted. The allowance varies with the type of sail and with the sailmaker concerned, but it is in the order of 2 or 3 per cent. The tack eye is worked into the sail and the luff is pulled until the cloth stretches the full distance along the wire. The head is then seized at its stretched position and the sail made fast to the head eye, so that the induced draft lies along the luff as a fold. If this seizing is released, the sail will fall back along the wire, and the draft will disappear into the bunt of the sail.

The exact amount which the sail is pulled depends on a number of factors, including the weight and quality of the cloth, the type and role of the sail, the size of the winch which will be used for the sheet and whether the sail should be full or flat. The sail may then either be seized at intervals along the luff wire, which is sewn close up all along its length so that it lies at the outer edge of the tabling at all times, or else the wire is left to lie freely inside the luff tabling. In either case, when the headsail is spread on the floor without pulling the wire taut, the wire will lie in a series of S-bends, either taking the luff with it, or else lying loose inside the tabling. This is because the cloth will only spread to a certain size and the wire, being longer, must zigzag to stay confined within the length of the unstretched luff. Not until the wire is pulled taut (with probably more tension than you can produce by hand – it needs its halyard) will the luff of the sail stretch to its designed length, producing induced draft as it goes.

Lay of the Panels

Because sailcloth stretches as soon as the strain is even the slightest bit on the bias, the sailmaker has to pay great attention to the way in which he lays the panels of a sail. Cloth stretch is the greatest single factor to be considered when making sails. By manipulating his panels so that the strain is either on or off the threadline as required, the sail-maker can control how much a sail stretches in a particular place. This is specially important in mainsail and headsail leeches and in spinnakers. Similarly, the faulty lay of a panel by as little as 1 or 2 degrees can upset the shape of a sail and, where this alignment is out by as much as 5 degrees, the sail can become virtually useless; we shall see the importance of this when we come to alterations to a sail which affect the angle at which the panels strike the leech. This explains why most leeches have seams running away from them approximately at right angles, since stretch on this part of the sail is undesirable, and the threadline must be followed. The panels are therefore often rocked or tripped round the roach of a mainsail or the hollow of a headsail so that the weft follows approximately the line of the leech.

Spreading a Sail

When sailmakers talk about spreading a sail, they mean laying it out on the loft floor as flat as possible – usually with the starboard side up – with the three sides under moderate tension and the rounds spread out so that the shape of the sail as cut out can be seen. This is done to a sail in the course of its manufacture, and before the rope or wire is fitted, so that the final shaping can be checked, or to

Plate 1. **Spreading a Sail.** *The white mainsail has been spread on W. G. Lucas and Son's loft floor (note the prickers at each corner); the darker sail has merely been laid on top for comparison. They are both for the same size of boat – the larger being for one of the 14-ft dinghies used in Bermuda.* Eastland.

a sail in for examination, so that an idea of its general shape and likely characteristics can be reached. To spread a sail properly requires the use of spikes, or prickers (awls or small screwdrivers with the tips sharpened to a point), which are pushed through the sail – at eyes or cringles wherever possible, but through the rope or even the sail itself if nothing else offers – and then into the floor. This may not be easy for the amateur sailmaker (think of the living-room carpet, not to mention your wife's temper) but, if you are ever going to tackle anything like major surgery on your sails, here and there in this book I shall have to assume that it is possible for you to use an attic or other wooden floor in this way without incurring somebody's wrath. An alternative is to use heavy weights to hold the sail out flat, but these are not so secure as prickers and they tend to be clumsy and get in the way. They also do not enable twine to be stretched round the three corners.

Twine. When any sail is spread, it may be desired to check the exact amounts of round or hollow to the luff, leech or foot. Take a length of twine or cord with a loop at one end, and put the loop over the pricker at the tack. Stretch this twine tight up to the head and put a half hitch over the pricker there, followed by the same at the clew and then back to the tack again. You now have the basic triangle of the sail, and a datum from which to work.

Mainsail. The boltrope or tape on the luff and foot of a mainsail restricts the natural deployment of the cloth, and you will find that you have to persuade the sail to take up its proper shape. Put a pricker through the tack eye and make sure it is firmly in the floor. Then pull the sail out on the luff, hard enough to remove most of the wrinkles from the sail near the rope, but not so hard as to cause too big a fold to appear just behind the luff; pricker it down through the head eye. Now do the same for the foot and then stretch the twine round so that the sail is basically spread. But you will find that you can adjust the cloth to either side of the twine by simply pulling it back and forth. It is a matter of experience to decide when the sail is lying naturally, but close inspection of the weft will usually help decide when there is no distortion. When you have the correct

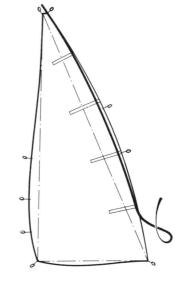

9. **Spreading a Mainsail**. *Pricker the three corners firmly into the floor, pulling luff and foot hard enough to remove most of the wrinkles next to the rope or tape (this may take more effort than you would imagine). Stretch twine all round this basic triangle and adjust the luff round so that it shows outside the twine; pricker down. Pull the leech across and stick a couple of prickers through the tabling into the floor. The sail in the drawing has been spread for roach reduction, and a webbing or linen tape has been 'thrown' along the line of the new leech ready for marking.*

amount of luff and foot round, stick a pricker into the floor through the boltrope at the points of maximum round; this will decide the amount of leech roach present (fig. 9).

If you really need to know the *exact* amount of round on the three edges of a mainsail, possibly to reduce or increase it, you must first take off the boltrope. Released from its constriction, the sail will then fall naturally into place without trouble, and you will be able to spread it easily and exactly.

Jib. A wire luff jib is easier than a mainsail to spread. Pull the wire out until it is as tight as possible and pricker both ends; then pull out the clew. The variation possible is not great, and the sail will lie evenly once the luff is pulled tight – but you should check that the wire is not still lying slack inside the luff tabling.

Spinnaker. Due to its almost hemispherical shape, a spinnaker may appear awkward to spread on a flat floor. But if it is folded in half down the middle, so that the two clews lie one on top of the other, the sail will lie substantially flat. Pricker the head eye firmly to the ground, and then pull out the two clews to the full extent of the leeches and pricker them down together. Now take the middle of the foot and pull it out, before prickering it down through the foot tape. Join the three prickers with twine or cord as before, and you can then adjust the leeches to one side and the middle of the sail to the other. Prickers should be stuck through the leeches at half and three-quarter height, and the cloth in the middle should be lightly tensioned across the sail and prickers put through the fold to hold it tight, taking care not to tear the sail.

Tablings

A tabling is an important part of the makeup of a sail. It is the hem turned over to reinforce the edge, and a proper understanding of its role is useful.

Heavy duty sails need a stout tabling to prevent the leech and foot from stretching too much. Lighter sails should have a narrow tabling, so that both tabling and leech or foot can stretch equally but within limits. If a sail has panels arriving at the free edge on the bias, a wider tabling will stop too much stretch, but it should not be so wide that there is noticeably less stretch of tabling than the cloth underneath it. If this occurs, the sail will form a bag just inside the tabling, but will be tight at the very edge. Certain dinghy sails can do away with the tabling altogether, leaving the leech and, less commonly, the foot with a heat-sealed raw edge. Such an edge will never curl through being too tight, but might easily go slack (apart from the problems it may experience from frayed ends).

Cut Tabling. The luffs of most mainsails and jibs have panels arriving at an appreciable angle. We know that sailcloth elongates on the bias so, if we want to keep stretch up the luff constant, we should avoid any alteration of this angle in forming the tabling. This means that the edge of the sail should not simply be folded over to form the hem, because this would double the bias angle at the luff; it must be cut off, lifted on to the sail and sewn back on again without being turned over (fig. 10). The effect of this is to keep the threadlines in the sail and the tabling parallel to one another. It takes a little longer than folding, and means that there are two rows of stitching down the edge of the sail instead of one, one of which runs right along the outside edge. This can become significant in the case of a wire luff jib if this particular row of stitches gets weakened and starts to give way (see Chapter 5).

Rolled Tabling. There is no harm in forming the tabling by folding or rolling the hem, when the cloth threadlines run parallel and at right angles to the edge of the sail in question (fig. 11). In this way there is no change in bias angle, the operation is simple and there are few stitches to cause trouble later. It is par-

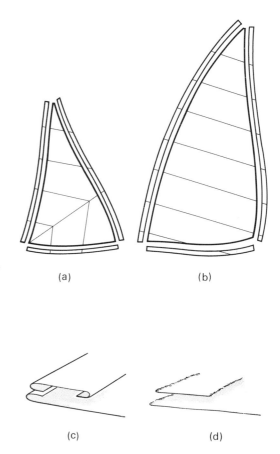

(a) (b)

(c) (d)

10. **Cut Tabling.** *All curves fit exactly and the threadlines, particularly at the luff, coincide when the tabling is lifted straight back on to the sail. The system leads to four thicknesses if the edges have to be turned under (c) instead of being heat sealed (d).*

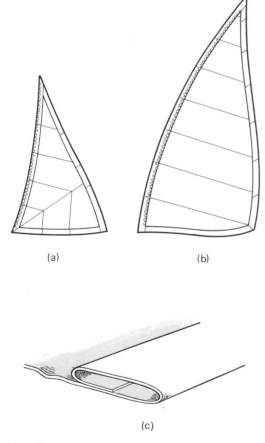

(a)

(b)

(c)

*11. **Rolled Tabling**. A rolled tabling with round or hollow will tend to gather in small puckers if the curve is at all marked; note how the bias angle at the luff changes. But there is much less stitching involved and it is lighter – an important factor at times.*

ticularly suited to light weather sails and those for dinghies, which have tablings only about half an inch wide. Some sails have rolled tablings all round, regardless of thread-line, and you will find small girts running off those which are on the doubled bias, due to the changed angle we have discussed.

Tape Tabling. The different stretch characteristics of a rolled tabling can be avoided by the use of Terylene or Dacron tape. It tends to be heavier than sailcloth, however, so it is best suited to the luff of a sail (and the foot of a mainsail) which, as we have already seen, is where conflicting bias angles are most likely to occur. It is easy to attach, and is folded in half down the middle and sewn to each side of the sail. A rope or wire can easily be enclosed in the tape before it is attached to the sail if desired (see Appendix B).

Rubbing Down

When a piece of sailcloth has to be folded and sewn, as with a tabling, it can be given its shape and marked for sewing by creasing along the line in question. This is called rubbing down, and it is also done to a sail which has reached the stage of having all its panels sewn together, so that ragged ends are left, but the sail is roughly the correct size; rubbing down is the final shaping to its exact dimensions. There have been special tools for this job down the centuries, but any hard flat surface will do, such as the handle of a knife or the back of a pair of scissors.

You can rub down to a line marked on the floor underneath the sail, to one marked in pencil on the cloth itself, or else to a row of holes pricked along the cloth to form the line in question. If a sail has to be reshaped at the luff, for example, the rope is taken off, then the tabling unpicked and finally the line of the luff round is rerubbed – either fuller or flatter as required. The resulting crease is then used as the mark to sew to.

Throwing a Tape

If the edge of a sail, spread without its rope or wire, has to be given a fair curve, it is done by marking two or three datum points (usually in relation to the straight twine) and then joining them by eye. To mark in a leech roach, a webbing tape or soft linen tape measure is anchored at the head and the tape 'thrown' to lie along the curve of the required roach, passing through the appropriate datum points. This is a matter of judgement and, like many jobs connected with sailmaking, the description is an anomaly; far from being thrown, the tape is laid carefully and meticulously (fig. 9).

three

Care of Sails in Use

Sail maintenance starts with the proper care of them during their normal use. The correct handling, stowing, cleaning and storing of sails will not only ensure their long life, but will also see that they are kept in good shape to do their job properly. Prevention is better than cure.

Handling

In Chapter 1 we saw the vulnerability of any woven material to bias stretch, and this must be constantly borne in mind when handling sails. Leeches in particular are open to excessive stretch if they are subjected to abnormal strain because, unlike luffs, they are unsupported by rope, wire or tape. Therefore the first point to remember is never to pull on leeches by hand.

Elementary, you say. But one of the most common sins of mishandling, committed hundreds of times a day by sailors of every standing and experience, is to pull jibs down by the leech. Repeated treatment of this kind will cause localised stretching of the cloth, resulting in a juddering leech needing the attentions of a sailmaker. The first lesson, therefore, is to pay more than lip-service to the cardinal rule which we all learned as soon as we started sailing: never pull on a leech.

Still on the subject of leeches, the mainsail has its own problems as it is being hoisted. Always support the main boom as the halyard is hauled, either by the topping lift or by hand, or else the weight of the boom, coupled with the flogging of the sail as it goes up, will overstress the leech.

Try to avoid point loading wherever it may occur. A genoa clew pulled too hard down over the lifeline, a mainsail which is allowed to bear too hard on the spreader ends, a spinnaker pole which is poked vigorously into the jib foot, can all cause localised stretching which will never recover. These are obvious examples, but a similar kind of problem can arise from treading on a sail which is lying over the engine control levers in a cockpit or is in the bottom of a dinghy, or in pulling too hard on a sail which has got caught up inside its bag.

Also under the category of mishandling is too harsh use of sheets, principally with headsails. This will overstretch the clew and may also affect the leech or foot, depending on the sheeting angle. But by far the most common distortion in use is caused by holding on to light-weather sails as the wind gets up above the strength for which they were designed. When a boat is going well under light genoa, and the wind gradually increases, the temptation is to leave well alone.

'She's going like a bomb, so it seems a pity to change down right at this moment.'

This will result in the light cloth being subjected to increasing loadings, so that the weave is finally distorted beyond the yield point. The draft is forced towards the leech, the sail bellies and backwinds the mainsail, and the boat will never again go properly to windward with that sail in that condition.

Chafe. We shall see later, when dealing with direct sail repairs, that chafe is one of the main bugbears of the sailing man. When sails bear against standing or running rigging, ropes or wires, spars or upperworks, movement of the boat will cause the harder of the two surfaces in contact to chafe the softer. When you remember the delicate nature of stitching and the fact that it does not bed into synthetic cloth as it used to in the days of cotton, but sits proud and exposed on the surface, it is not difficult to guess which is going to be damaged. Indeed most, if not all, of the objects mentioned above are also harder than the sailcloth itself, so not only the stitching will wear. The damage can start after quite a short time, and the size of the problem and the extensive precautions which have to be taken can be surprising to the man who has never done any serious blue-water cruising. Baggy-wrinkle anti-chafe is not for the birds. The points to watch for in particular are as follows:

Plate 2. **Chafe.** *A jib can quickly chafe stitching if the foot bears on the pulpit or lifeline when off the wind.* Author.

Mainsails. Lee shrouds and spreaders when running free; a slack topping lift, left attached to the outer end of the boom; running or adjustable backstays which are not carried right forward on the lee side; battens at both ends of the pockets; the part of the sail which runs in the mast, boom or stay groove, particularly at the head and, in the case of mainsails, the clew.

Jibs. The leech of overlapping headsails on the lee shrouds, jumper stays and spreader ends when closehauled (split tennis balls on the ends of spreaders are quick to fit, cheap and effective); the foot where it passes over the pulpit or lifeline when off the wind, and where it bears against the lee shroud when going to windward (wrap shroud turnbuckles in tape, particularly if they have split pins); the leech where it chafes the mast on going about (the clew is particularly vulnerable).

Spinnakers. The foot which bears on the forestay on a dead run if it is kept too tightly sheeted; the clew in the same way on a reach; the head through the action of the swivel working from side to side and collapsing in light winds, particularly if the swivel is shackled on and is thus slack.

Not all the above are avoidable, for instance nothing can be done about battens chafing their pockets, or the genoa foot fouling the pulpit. But they all give rise to trouble from time to time and, if you can't retrim or rig shockcord to avoid them, they show you what to look for when examining for wear and tear.

Stowing

You may be tempted to think that no harm can come to your sails once they are safely down and not subjected to the wind. True, they will not chafe but they can be creased or torn, or even weakened by the effect of sunlight or industrial smoke.

The problem of bagging sails is, of course, one of creases. I am speaking here purely in the light of sail care and not as regards bagging a sail from the point of how best to have it ready for the next time it has to be used; the two are not necessarily incompatible. Polyester sailcloth to which a lot of chemical fillers have been added in the finishing stage will crease more readily than a softer material with less dressing in it. The modern tendency towards the latter finish, therefore, considerably lessens the danger. In addition, a cloth of under about 5 ounces will crease more readily than a heavier one, and the lighter winds to which these sails are normally exposed will not blow the creases out again. Nylon is a soft elastic material, so spinnakers are not prone to this problem (which is fortunate, considering the way they are bunched into turtles and launching tubes).

Straightforward stuffing of a sail into a sailbag can therefore be better accepted for a heavier cloth, or for one of the softer materials. Even so, the bag should be large enough to avoid having to compress the sail too tightly. Don't forget to see that the result has plenty of room in the sail locker, and that it does not get covered by the spare anchor or a couple of heavy mooring lines – all of which will cause creases through the bag.

Sails for boats up to about the size of a one-design day sailer, such as the Dragon or

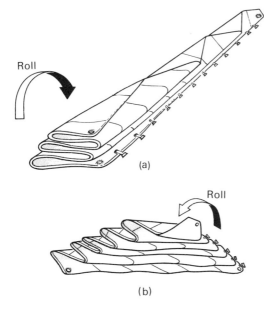

(a)

(b)

12. **Folding a Mainsail**. *A mainsail is best folded by two people, one working along each edge. The creases will be vertical in (a) and horizontal in (b).*

Soling, can be folded with advantage and without too much inconvenience. A mainsail should be flaked back and forth, either horizontally or vertically (if you do it alternate ways each week, the risk of establishing a permanent crease will be reduced), and then rolled to suitable size (fig. 12). A dinghy mainsail is stowed virtually without creases at all

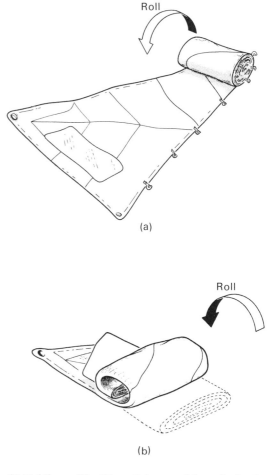

(a)

(b)

13. **Folding a Jib**. *The roll is started from the head, down the luff (a). The completed roll is then rolled again from luff to clew (b).*

by rolling it round its own boom. A headsail should be rolled into a hoop along its own luff wire from head to tack, then rolled again from the luff towards the clew. Any window can usually be arranged to come at a place where it will not be folded or rolled too tightly (fig. 13).

Take particular care to see that leeches are free from accidental creasing or repeated folds in the same place. If your time and patience will only extend to folding one headsail from a large wardrobe, attend to the light-weather sail. This will usually be made of cloth around 2 to 4 ounces, which is easily creased. It goes without saying that you should be particularly careful with lighted cigarettes while all this is going on.

Sail Covers. Ultraviolet rays and certain industrial chemicals can degrade synthetic sailcloth, both polyester (Terylene or Dacron) and nylon, to the point where it becomes brittle and will tear like paper. Sails should therefore be protected from prolonged exposure to sunlight or smoke (I am talking here about a year's constant exposure). This means regular use of covers for those sails which are left on their spars at sunny moorings, such as mainsail, mizzen or boom staysail. Jibs which are regularly left rolled up on the fore-stay, or mainsails which are flaked on the boom with the foot pulled

out to form a neat parcel round the rest of the sail in a shipshape spit-and-polish stow will continually expose the same part of the sail to the elements. Being the most delicate component, it is the stitching which once again goes first, and the mainsail foot or the jib leech and foot will quickly become weak spots; after the stitching starts to go, the cloth itself will weaken and easily tear. A good cover, therefore, will quickly pay its way. To be good, a cover should be water- and lightproof, yet should allow the sail to breathe to avoid condensation. This means that it should not be too tight fitting underneath. As covers are important in sunny climates, acrylic material (which 'breathes' but does not rot) is particularly suitable, but it is flammable so be warned; plastic-coated synthetic cloth is also often used. The cover should go right round the mast at the forward end, with a tight collar at the top. A lacing is probably best for the attachment to the mast, as it can then be pulled really tight; shock cord and hooks, or Velcro are the quickest way along the underside of the cover. The inconvenience of catching lines and clothing on hooks, if they are placed on the outside, should be weighed against the way they will scratch the boom if placed inside. I prefer the former alternative, but the choice is marginal, particularly if the cover is nice and free-hanging underneath the boom.

Washing

During the course of a season, sails can pick up a wide variety of stains which not only makes them unsightly, but can also harm the sails themselves. Even sea water leaves a deposit of salt on the surface, which proceeds to work its way into the weave, there to act as an abrasive by sawing away at the threads and weakening the material. All sails should therefore be regularly washed in fresh water, with special attention being paid when the boat is laid up for the winter.

It will be difficult for the owner himself to wash thoroughly sails for anything larger than a day sailer or a trailerboat. Regular hosing down at the marina berth will repay the effort, as a large buildup of salt will be avoided this way. Hoist the sail up the mast by the tack to dry, taking care to see that it blows freely to leeward without fouling on anything. In this way the largest part of the sail will be well up the mast, with the usually narrow head coming down to the deck; attach a line to the head to make it secure. I include spinnakers in this generalisation.

Owners of dinghies are quite used to this routine, and they usually rinse down in the dinghy park, both hull and sails, at the end of the day. The man with a small keelboat, possibly left on an offshore mooring, can be at a slight disadvantage, because he may not have

Plate 3. **Drying Ashore.** *Hung by the luff, this sail will not stretch its leech.* Author.

easy access to a hose. But a special trip to the marina or dinghy park is not much to ask, or else the sails can be taken home and spread under the hose on the lawn or a clean concrete apron, in which case you may use a broom or scrubbing brush with a little liquid detergent, providing you rinse it out.

When washing on concrete or other rough surfaces, take care that you are not too energetic, for you can chafe the stitching against the ground underneath, and you may also remove some of the protective silicone coating which helps keep the cloth smooth and repels moisture.

When hanging up to dry, see that weight is not taken on the leech, which would thus stretch out of shape. Hang by the head or tack, so that the luff takes the strain, and don't leave the sail flogging in the wind for too long. Even if it is not chafing on any obvious obstruction, it will be steadily rubbing against itself and thus weakening the stitching (fig. 14).

Cleaning

I differentiate between washing and cleaning as between the routine rinse to clean off any salt after a wet trip, and the final cleaning of sails before they are put away for the winter at the end of the season. This will also take account of any specific stains such as varnish, blood, paint etc., although these should normally be cleaned off as soon as they occur and not be allowed to harden over a period of weeks. The advice on cleaning various stains given below is based largely on information kindly supplied by ICI Fibres, of England,

14. **Hanging Sails to Dry**. *Sails should be hung to dry so that their weight is supported by the luff, which has reinforcement in the shape of wire, rope or tape.*

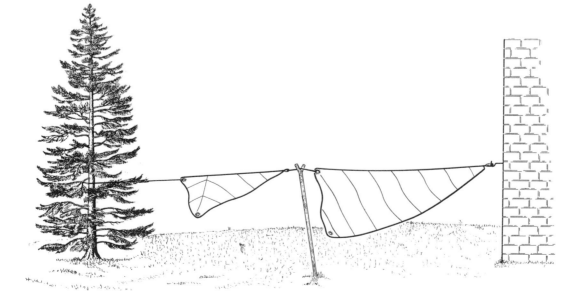

which refers specifically to white Terylene but is also applicable to Dacron; dyed sails often need individual treatment by specialist dry cleaners or finishers (beware, for instance, of using bleaching agents or solvents, and don't use bleach on nylon of any kind). Never use galvanised or alloy containers, but stick to stainless steel or polythene (or porcelain or enamel, if they are not chipped).

Many of the chemicals specified can be bought at a druggist. Keep strong ones away from all metal parts of the sail and always rinse out after treatment, if only to remove the danger of a 'high water mark' on the cloth. Avoid getting chemicals on the skin, in the eyes or in the lungs; wash skin and clothes thoroughly if affected.

While some of these processes are harmless enough, get into the habit of treating them all as dangerous. Make sure that you have plenty of fresh air and avoid fire risks, not only for the obvious reasons but also because some of these chemicals can give off poisonous gases when their vapour is drawn through a lighted cigarette (chlorinated solvents, for instance, produce phosgene gas in this way). So don't smoke.

Alkalis can make polyester cloth more sensitive to the weakening effect of ultraviolet rays, while acids do the same for nylon. The warning here is to avoid alkali-based detergents for washing Terylene or Dacron if you cannot spend time to rinse out afterwards, and keep materials with a high acid content off spinnakers. Detergent powders are frequently alkali-based but they may, in fact, be used if you rinse well afterwards; liquid detergents are less likely to have alkalis in them because they are usually what is known as 'soapless' detergents. Soapless detergents (either liquid or powder) are equally efficient in hard, soft or even salt water. They are neutral in solution so, being neither acid nor alkali based, are suitable for both polyester and nylon sails. Acid and alkali can be measured by the pH scale (potential of hydrogen). When a pH test paper is dipped into the detergent solution, it changes colour and can be compared with a graded chart from which the pH value can be read. A chart value of pH 7 is exactly neutral, with values below 7 becoming progressively more acidic and those above being alkaline. Before leaving this subject I must repeat that the overall effect of alkalis can easily be neutralised by rinsing in fresh water; in any event the problem is minimal and should be kept in perspective.

Finally I must add that, while the various treatments set forth in this book are given in all good faith, my publishers, ICI Fibres and I cannot accept responsibility for any damage which may result from following them.

Wash. Large sails should be spread on a clean concrete apron and washed with hot water, using bar soap or detergent. Any sail which can be got into the bath (less than about 150 square feet) should be immersed in water as hot as the hand can stand (50° C, or 120° F), and similarly treated. A sailmaker would probably use a none-too-gentle industrial rotary scrubber so, if you are working on a reasonably smooth surface, don't be afraid to work hard at it. A smooth base will ensure that the effects of chafe are minimal but, in any case, you should not rub away at one particular patch of stitching for more than about quarter of a minute. If you cannot get rid of local areas of particularly heavy dirt, soak the patch overnight in straight detergent. If general soiling is still hard to remove, soak in a mixture of sodium metasilicate and cold water (1 lb to 1 gallon); do not allow the solution to come into contact with galvanised luff wires, alloy slides, bronze thimbles, snap hooks or piston hanks. Then drain the sail, wash in detergent and rinse. As an alternative, you could put up to 6 ounces of sodium hydroxide (caustic soda) into a bath full of water and soak it in that; don't increase the proportion. If you decide to wash the sail in a machine, keep your eye on the water temperature to see that it does not get above hand heat, or it may cause localised distortion.

Adhesive Numbers. It can sometimes be difficult to remove completely all trace of adhesives used with stick-on sail numbers. Steam the number in question over a bowl of hot water to start it peeling, and then brush it with a sponge soaked in a solvent/detergent mixture such as Polyclens or Mr Clean. An alternative is to soak for a while in toluene, or overnight in one of the biological soap powders. Rinse thoroughly afterwards whichever method is used.

Blood. Blood will respond to soaking in one of the biological soap powders. There is a slight danger that optical brighteners may react with dyestuffs, some special resins and also some ropes, so use a powder without brighteners if you can find one. Keep adhesive numbers out of the solution or they may come off; this is particularly true when the sail is left to soak for long periods (overnight) for the enzymes to 'digest' the protein. Really stubborn bloodstains can be attacked by soaking in a 5 per cent solution of ammonia and water (one cupful of ammonia to each gallon of water). If this doesn't work, damp the stain with a 1 per cent solution of pepsin in water acidified with a few drops of dilute hydrochloric acid (spirits of salt), allow to stand without drying out for 30 minutes and then rinse thoroughly.

Mildew. Scrub lightly with a stiff dry brush to remove as much of the surface mildew as possible, then soak for a couple of hours in a cold solution of bleach (sodium hypochlorite) at a strength of approximately 1 per cent available chlorine, or use one part of domestic bleach such as Domestos, Brobat or Clorox to ten parts of water (a cupful to half a gallon); rinse afterwards and be prepared for only partial success. Don't use bleach on nylon. Any remaining smell of chlorine can be removed by dipping for a few minutes in a 1 per cent solution of sodium thiosulphate (photographer's hypo). Rinse with fresh water.

Oil, Grease and Wax. Small stains of this nature can be removed by dabbing with a proprietary carbon tetrachloride stain remover such as Thawpit, Dabitoff, Energine or Renuzit; rinse after treatment. Heavy staining is best attacked by brushing on an industrial hand-cleansing gel (such as Swarfega, Palmit, the American Flash or 745), or a mixture of solvent (stain remover or toluene) and detergent in a ratio of 2 : 1; leave for about 15 minutes and then wash off with warm water. You can also use Polyclens, which is a proprietary solvent/detergent mixture. These treatments will remove oils, greases, petroleum jelly and most lubricating mixtures, but they will not remove stains caused by the metallic particles often associated with lubricants. Such stains can best be tackled by the methods described below, after the oil and grease have been eliminated.

Metallic Stains. Stains caused by metals, in the form of rust, verdigris or finely divided particles, can be removed by either of the following methods (do not allow the solutions to come into contact with galvanised iron, bronze or copper):

1. Immerse the stained portion in a 5 per cent solution of oxalic acid – salts of lemon – dissolved in hot water (1 ounce of oxalic acid to each pint of hot water). The hands and the sail should be washed very thoroughly after using oxalic solutions, as this chemical is poisonous.

2. Immerse the stained portion in a warm solution containing two parts of concentrated hydrochloric acid per 100 parts of water. Wash off thoroughly with fresh water.

Pitch and Tar. Organic solvents such as perchloroethylene, trichloroethylene, trichloroethane (Genklene), solvent naphtha or white or mineral spirits may be dabbed on to the stain to effect removal. Again, care should be taken to work in a well-ventilated position, and due precautions should be taken when working with flammable solvents. The easiest household cure to find is probably one of the hand cleansing gels; brush it on, leave for 15 minutes and then rinse off with hot water.

Paint. Turpentine substitute, or mineral or white spirits will do as good a job as any on soft paint, but dry paint is hard to remove. Avoid paint strippers which are based on alkalis (and most are) but, if turps substitute or spirits don't work, try chloroform.

Varnish. Treatment of varnish is much the same as paint: turps sub or white/mineral spirits when wet, and liquid chloroform for dry polyurethane varnish; try using pure alcohol or methylated spirits for dry shellac varnish. If desperate, dab the stain first with trichloroethylene and then with a mixture of equal parts of acetone and amyl acetate. In any event, rinse with fresh water at the finish.

Ironing

The best advice to those who want to know about ironing sails is *Don't*. But many owners get rid of persistent creases successfully in this way and thereby encourage others to follow suit, so a few words on the subject seem to be in order. The creases which lend themselves best to elimination by ironing are those which sometimes settle in the leech, causing the tabling to sit up at right angles and flutter in the wind with a characteristic 'motorboating' noise. Extreme heat will melt synthetic cloth, and even a temperature of 70° C (160° F) will cause uneven shrinkage producing local hard spots, so be warned. Use an electric iron on its lowest setting, switch it off before starting and don't leave it in contact with the same part of the sail for longer than two or three seconds. Above all, be prepared for the treatment to ruin the sail for all time.

Winter Storing

Sails should be stored loosely flaked in a clean dry room or garage, so that air can circulate freely; the truly conscientious will turn them over once or twice during the winter. If nothing else, this should reveal if they have been eaten by rats or mice (whether they actually eat the cloth, or merely use it to make their nests, they seem to have a liking for sails, and the result is the same whatever they do with the material).

These conditions are the ideal ones, and I am aware that they do not always occur. The main thing to remember is no damp and no creases, therefore any dry place will do, and the sails may be stored in their bags if these are big enough to avoid having to cram the sails into them. Dinghy sails can often be stored rolled round the main boom and hoisted on to the rafters of the garage. At all events, avoid folding or bunching sails too tightly, and do not put heavy weights on top of them. See that windows are not folded or creased.

Note of Hope

The above warnings may be intimidating, but fortunately polyester and nylon are robust modern materials and extremely forgiving. Sail care should be kept in perspective and, with reasonable precautions, you should get years of service from your boat's wardrobe – but the more careful you are the more service you will get, so don't overdo the harsh treatment too often.

four

Examination for Repairs

We have just seen in Chapter 3 how important it is to look into the proper care of sails before we could discuss the question of how to repair them. Even then, we had to find out how to handle them prior to going on to cleaning and storing. Now we must learn how to examine a sail for damage, as opposed to faults in set, before getting down to the repair proper.

The first advice I must give you is not to be afraid of being a bit ruthless. If a seam is suspect, don't pick at it half-heartedly or it may not show its weakness. Have a good pull at individual stitches with your fingernails and, if any of the thread breaks, get the back of a knife or the point of a nail file on to it; now is the time that you want to find anything which is going to let you down, not when you are afloat. Go right along a suspect seam vigorously, pulling stitches at intervals, to find out the full extent of any weakness. I am not, of course, advocating wholesale unpicking of stitches, because even weak thread will help hold a seam together with the addition of the new stitches you will put in. Similarly, scratch hard all round a tear or chafe mark until you find where it starts to have strength again, because it is no good leaving weak cloth next to a new patch – it will only tear again.

Put on a pair of clean soft shoes, or take your shoes off altogether, because you are going to walk and kneel all over the sail. The other preparation you should make is to thread a needle with any twine which contrasts with the sail: red for a white sail, white for a tan or blue sail. The type of thread is immaterial, because it is only going to be used to mark the repair and will later be discarded.

Organise the examination systematically, starting perhaps at the head and working your way round and across the sail.

Mainsails

Spread the sail loosely on the ground, indoors if possible, even if it means doing it by halves.

Head. Look at the headboard itself to see whether the rivets are firm, the stitching sound and the headboard unbroken. Check the eye where the halyard is shackled, to see if there is any undue wear or distortion. If the mast has a luff groove, the cloth between the boltrope and the headboard may be worn; if it has a track, how are the slides on the headboard? There should be two slides here on a boat of any size, so think about adding a second if there is only one.

Luff. Now go all down the luff, checking slides for firm and even attachment, together with undistorted eyelets, and also looking at the tabling to see that the stitching is sound. Are there any signs of chafe near the bolt-rope? Look carefully at any reef cringles for distortion.

Tack. The tack, of course, is subjected to great strain, because it is pulled by the hal-yard and also by the clew outhaul. It may well be a hand-worked eye, with a brass liner, but in some sails it may be an eye punched in by a sophisticated machine, with a steel liner. Look at it critically for distortion or possibly for breakage of any hand stitches round the eye; the boltrope itself may show signs of chafe here if it rubs against the boom under the influence of too short a shackle. This is also the time to look at the Cunningham hole if one is fitted (or, if not, to mark the place to put one of these simple, cheap and most ef-fective devices).

Foot. The foot should receive the same sort of examination as the luff: slides, eyelets, chafe in the groove and broken stiches in the tabling. If you have roller reefing and any projections on the boom, such as a vang at-tachment, which could chafe the sail when it is rolled round the boom, check on any wear which may be apparent slightly in towards the middle of the sail (i.e. at the first roll). Finally, include any slab reef arrangements in

this: zippers for missing teeth or stitching starting to chafe, the slider for rust or distor-tion, or lacing holes for signs of strain.

Clew. The clew is vulnerable. Check the liner of the eye for distortion or cracks, the stitching of the eye for breakages and the sail immediately under the eye for chafe or tears. There is often a leather or canvas protection over the boltrope at the clew; see that it is firmly attached and free from chafe or tears, and that it is not hiding a weak spot in the cloth underneath it. If there is no casing, this might explain why the boltrope has a ten-dency to pull out of the boom groove; fit one and the extra thickness might stop this trouble. If the sail is fitted with slides along the foot, see whether one could be fitted to the clew eye itself without interfering with the outhaul, and mark it if appropriate. Check the boltrope for firm attachment, either finishing abruptly at the end of the foot if it runs in a groove, or else being tailed round the corner and a few inches up the leech if the boom has a track.

Leech. The leechline will emerge from the tabling just above the clew; examine the eyelets for firmness. Is there any quick way of fastening the line? If not, note it down for attention (see Chapter 6). Next, run up the leech, looking carefully at the tabling where it

Plate 4. **Laid out for Checkover.** *Spread loosely on the ground, this jib can now be examined all over. Note how the wire luff lies in twists because it is not under tension to stretch the cloth.* Author.

can chafe on adjustable running backstays, topping lift or spinnaker sheets. This is a prolific source of repairs, and you should be ready for a good deal of weak or broken stitching. The outer ends of batten pockets are particularly liable to chafe, not only from the batten itself, but because the batten offers a hard base to help sandwich the sail with any loose wire or line. See if the upper end of the leechline is firmly anchored to the leech at the aft end of the headboard.

Bunt of the Sail. We saw in Chapter 3 the principal ways in which a mainsail can be chafed; now is the time to put that knowledge into practice. Look all over the sail for signs of chafe, with particular attention being paid to the stitching at the seams. There will be a band of vulnerability which runs up from the foot parallel to the luff, where the sail rubs against the shrouds when running before the wind; this will almost certainly be denoted by metallic staining picked up from the wire itself. Examine any reef points and don't forget the sail numbers.

Headsails

The same kind of operation should be carried out on headsails.

Head. See that the head eye is undisturbed and that the seizing which lashes the luff to the eye is intact underneath its casing. If the sail is made for a groove, check on the cleanness of the entry and for signs of chafe on the cloth itself.

Luff. Again look over as for a mainsail, substituting hanks or snap hooks for the slide check. If the sail has a wire luff, hold the bottom foot or so near the tack up to your ear and bend it back and forth, listening for the tell-tale rustle which reveals a stranded wire (the tack area, of course, is most liable to this trouble because it gets dunked frequently, and any plastic covering of the wire will have been disturbed by the formation of the eye and so can let in water). If the sail has a tabling which has been cut off the sail and replaced rather than rolled, there will be stitching right up the very front of the wire; this is a weak point, and you should pick hard at this stitching to see if it has begun to weaken. Check the function of all hanks and snap hooks.

Tack. Check for distortion of the eye, and to see whether salt water may have got through any plastic coating and started to corrode the wire. Have a good look at the reinforcing patches.

Foot. The foot can chafe against the shrouds or on the lifeline, so look carefully at the tabling. Check the drawstring of any headsail fitted with one of these along the foot.

Clew. The clew is the meeting point of many stresses, so look at the eye carefully for signs of distortion or wear. The clew reinforcement patches may chafe their stiches on the mast or shrouds at each tack, so this is an area which should not be missed.

Leech. Of all the parts of the many sails on a boat, possibly the most important is the genoa leech. We know all about the slot, turbulence and loss of thrust, but one of the other fields in which it also has an influence is on the morale of the helmsman. If part of the tabling has come unstitched, it will hammer in the wind like a stuttering machine-gun, causing the driver to start worrying and lose concentration. As it happens, the leech is particularly vulnerable to chafe, expecially on the shrouds and spreader ends, so look carefully all along it for broken stitches which can spell trouble unless they are oversewn quickly.

Bunt of the Sail. There should not be much chafe on the middle of a headsail, unless it is the jib of a cutter rig which has to drag across the inner forestay every time the boat tacks; in this case, there will be chafe everywhere, so be warned. Look also at any tell-tales or streamers which are fitted, ready to renew as necessary, and check for general tears and holes.

Spinnakers

Being more delicate than most other sails, a spinnaker can give a lot of practice to the amateur sailmaker. Take it into the garden on a quiet day (on the assumption that you don't have a big enough room at your disposal), so that you can spread it out for a good look.

Head. Look for distortion of the head eye, security of the swivel and signs of chafe on the stitching holding the patch, particularly if the swivel is attached with a shackle which allows it to move from side to side.

Clews. Here again, check the eyes for distortion and wear, and the patches for chafe.

Leeches. Tie the head to a tree about 6 to 8 feet above the ground and pull the clews out side by side to the full extent of the leeches. Compare them for length and, if one is longer than the other, something has broken (leech wires, if fitted, or tapes). You will have to find out what it is, and it will be a sail loft job for all but the more ambitious amateur. Go all down each leech, looking for chafe, particularly if the spinnaker has thin wires running inside the tapes because these can cause wear on the tape itself. At the same time take a good look at the very edge of the nylon, where the cloth has been slightly weakened by a row of machine stitching holding it to the tape; this is where a tear can start and it will lead to big trouble if it is not spotted in the very early stages.

Foot. This should have the same treatment as the leeches. Look carefully, for the foot sometimes rubs against the forestay so that the stitching gets chafed.

Bunt of the Sail. With the head still attached to the tree, hold each clew in turn as high as possible and pull on the leech, while you look through the sail into the light. This will quickly show up any seams which may have come unsewn or tears even as small as pinpricks. The middle of a spinnaker is, perhaps, the only part of a sail which you should not mark with contrasting thread, for the needle holes you make to do this are themselves not insignificant. Take hold of a fistful of nylon and bundle it into a knot with the tear at the end of it.

five

Typical Repairs – Basic Items

Seams

Seam repairs will always figure high on the repair list while Terylene and Dacron remains so hard that the machine stitching stays on the surface, open to the ravages of chafe. This is particularly true when you remember that the thread is also synthetic and, being of a fairly delicate nature, is the first to suffer from the weakening effects of the sun's ultraviolet rays.

Providing a seam only goes at the stitching, however, its repair does not present a particularly major problem. But once a seam has started to go, the sail is weakened at that point and other damage can occur. The sail may tear across the cloth, or the selvedge of the cloth may fray so that there is nothing solid for the new stitching to get hold of. 'A stitch in time saves nine' was never more true than when referring to a sail which has begun to show signs of chafe.

One of the best repair measures, therefore, is to catch things in their early stages before damage has really begun to show all over. If your examination shows that the stitching is weak here and there throughout the sail, with short lengths of a few inches broken where chafe has been particularly persistent, you may be sure that the thread has begun to weaken and needs reinforcing. A sail in this condition will almost certainly be four or five years old, and is ready for a third row of stitching to be put down the middle of every seam by sewing machine. This is a tedious but simple process, the two parts of the sail being already firmly lined up and held together; the most difficult part about the exercise is handling the bulk of the sail underneath the arm of the machine. Until you have got a good deal of practice, I suggest trying this yourself only if it is a question of a jib which is under about 20 feet on the luff.

If the sail is only about 2 or 3 years old and the bulk of the stitching can be considered to be in good heart, so that you cannot break it with your fingernails, but there are areas where chafe has caused 6 inches or so of seam to come undone, then the repair is best undertaken by hand. Providing you have caught it early enough, this should merely be a question of sewing the two parts together again.

If you are lucky, the seam will be sufficiently near the edge of the sail for you to be able to tackle it from both sides. I say this, despite the general instructions that seams should be sewn with the tabling or flat seaming stitch. When you can pass the needle back and forth through the canvas, you will be able to pick up the empty machine-stitch holes, thus making the job easier and also better looking (even a sailmaker's regular and even tabling stitches are going to look altogether

different from the zigzag pattern of the sewing machines although old machine-stitch
holes can also be used by the amateur to keep
flat seaming stitches regular). Start well into
the sound stitching so that there is a good
overlap and, when you have been once along
the repair, you will find that you have only
filled in the machine stitching at every other
stitch, even though you have passed the
needle through each hole. This is because the
machine applies thread to both sides of the
work at once, from two bobbins, whereas
with hand sewing you have only one source
of supply; the alternate stitches will be filled
in underneath the sail (fig. 15). There is no
need, however, to work your way back filling
in the gaps, unless you want to make the job
look smart. This is because you will be using
a waxed hand-seaming twine far stouter than
the machine thread it is replacing, and the
overall strength of your repair will almost
certainly be greater than the original.

If the seam is in the middle of a fairly
bulky sail, you will find that you will have to
get down to the flat seaming stitch described
in Appendix B. Turn the sail so that the lap of
the cloths is away from you, with the nearer
panel on top. Now start seaming from the
right as described in Appendix B; once again,
start four or five stitches into the good
thread. If there are two of you, it is still
possible to pick up the old machine stitches,

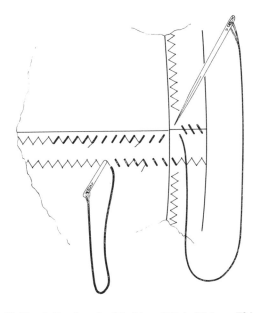

*15. **Hand Sewing in Machine Stitch Holes.** This
enables even a beginner to turn in a neat job. After going
along the seam once, only half the stitches will be covered
although all the holes are filled. Hand twine is so much
stronger than machine thread, however, that only the
fastidious need go back over it again to fill in the gaps.
Note also how the seams run across the tabling. Free
passage down the leech must be left whenever a leechline
is fitted, so take care not to sew right through the sail at
this point; the tabling stitch is mandatory here.*

by holding the sail up between you and passing the needle to each other back and forth
through the cloth.

Plate 5. **Hand Stitching in Machines Holes.** *It is not essential to go back over the seam a second time to fill in the gaps, because the doubled heavy twine is much stronger than the original machine stitching, but it makes the job look neater.* Jarman.

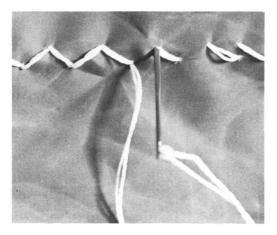

When you have finished the job, hammer it flat with your fist and remove the tally you put on when marking the sail during your examination.

If the torn seam is not spotted early in its life, the selvedge of one of the cloths may start to fray. This makes it difficult for the stitching to get a firm base on its original line, and you will have to sew further into the sail. First you must stop the fraying, and this is done by means of an electric soldering iron, used to seal the ends of the weft which are fraying. I should not need to tell you to be careful, first not to touch any other parts of the sail with the iron, and secondly not to be too enthusiastic about how much cloth you melt and fuse as you seal the edge. You must, of course, leave some sort of overlap between the two cloths, or you will find yourself having to put on a patch.

Where a small tear has started, possibly at right angles across the panel, because of the weakening effect of a torn seam, this should be mended before the seam is repaired. Anything up to two or three inches can be gathered together by the sailmaker's darn, as shown in Appendix B, providing the tear is clean. When the darn is complete, repair the seam as described above, making sure to space your stitches carefully as you seam across the tear. If the tear is large or ragged, possibly with frayed edges, you must put on a patch first. This is where self-adhesive sail patches pay off, for you can stick one on and then seam across the patch, without the end result being too bulky due to a double lot of stitching at the seam; sew round the rest of the patch for security after the seam is complete.

Tablings

As we have seen, tablings give a lot of trouble, particularly on headsails. The most frequent fault is for the stitching which holds the tabling to be broken. This releases an inch or so of sail at the leech or foot to flap in the breeze.

Resewing along the tabling parallel to the

leech or foot is no problem; it is done in the same way as a seam between two cloths in the sail, usually picking up the old stitch holes as you go. But the tabling is almost certainly formed by panels of cloth joined together, so that you get a join at least every three feet. What happens in these circumstances is that the joins part as well. Where a leechline is involved, the repair becomes a little more delicate because you must leave a clear passage all down the tabling without sewing right through the sail. You therefore have to mend each join (it is really the end of a seam joining two cloths or panels) by using the tabling stitch and taking great care that the point of your needle does not pick up the other side of the tabling as you go, thus sealing off the drawstring (fig. 15). If you use a delicate touch, you should with practice be able to feel or even hear the point of your needle as it pricks the second cloth below the one you are sewing. It has happened to many a so-called expert, however, that the drawstring itself is sewn permanently into the repair. . . .

Batten Pockets

There are two common repairs to batten pockets, one difficult and one easy. Let us deal with the easy one first.

This concerns the aftermost part of the pocket, where it joins the leech of the sail – the opening, in fact. Battens either rest in their pockets or, on many sails, they are forced towards the leech by elastic at the inner end. In either case, the hard nature of the batten combines with pressure and chafe to work away at the stitching which closes the outer end; repeated forcing as the batten is put in and taken out does nothing to help this stitching either.

The cure is to put a row of hand stitches along the very leech below the opening, using a stout twine. It is best to turn the sail so that it is starboard-side up and then begin sewing at the bottom of the batten opening, namely at the left of the work to be sewn. In this way, you can knot the twine as a stopper and hide the knot by sewing first between the layers of cloth through one side of the opening, then oversewing two or three stitches to hide the knot and to act as a strong reinforcement to the bottom of the batten opening. Continue sewing with the round stitch from left to right, evenly spaced, about five or six stitches to the inch. When you reach the end of the pocket closure, sew a couple of times over and over and finish off by sewing back through the last two or three stitches (fig. 16).

The more difficult of these two common repairs requires a patch. This usually occurs

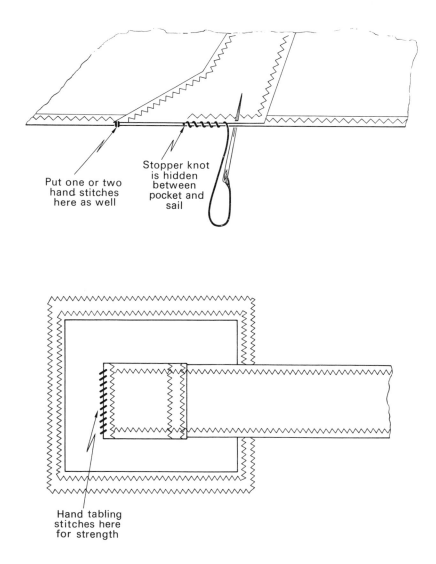

Stopper knot
is hidden
between
pocket and
sail

Put one or two
hand stitches
here as well

Hand tabling
stitches here
for strength

16. Reinforcing Batten Pockets (top). *This is an easy and worthwhile repair job, easily achieved. Note how the stopper knot is tucked away out of sight.*

17. Batten Pocket Patch (bottom). *A patch on the sail should be put on the opposite side to the pocket; one on the pocket itself should go outside rather than inside. This is not important, but it avoids the possibility of the batten end having to push against the second layer of cloth as it is inserted.*

at the inner end of the pocket and is caused by the batten end chafing the cloth inside the pocket. You have to unpick the stitching holding the inner end of the pocket to the sail for as far as is necessary, so that the last 6 inches or so hangs free from the sail; if there is an elastic insert to tension the batten against the leech, this must also be unpicked from the side which has to be patched. If it is the sail which has worn, it should be trimmed and patched in the usual way, putting the patch on the opposite side to the pocket, to stop the batten end catching in the seam. The pocket is then replaced, together with its elastic if appropriate. If it is the pocket which has chafed through, the end should be cut off and a new piece of cloth substituted to bring the pocket back to the correct length again; this should be double-sewn across and either turned under if the edge is unsealed or else burned off with an iron to match the original. The pocket is then resewn as before (fig. 17).

Patches

A clean cut of about an inch in length may be sewn together with a sailmaker's darn, providing the cloth is in good heart; anything larger should have a patch. If you can put one on in the old-fashioned way, by turning the raw edges of patch and sail under to form a tabling or hem, you will be ready for the worst case such as when you are afloat and have no soldering iron, or perhaps have no sticky tape or self-adhesive patches available.

A sail tear is often L-shaped. It must be squared up and repaired in the manner described in Appendix B. If the patch runs up to a seam, you must first unpick the seam for as far as is necessary, patch right to the edge of the cloth (using a selvedge or a heat-sealed edge on the patch to run along the seam), and then resew the seam. A tear which goes right across a seam should ideally be patched up to the seam on each side (i.e. two separate patches) and then reseamed, although the job will hold well enough if put on in one piece. If the tear is near to a boltrope or luff wire, take the patch right round the rope or wire and over both sides of the sail if the result will not be too bulky.

Chafing Piece. If a particular part of a sail is subject to unavoidable chafe, it is as well to patch it each side before it wears through. Candidates for this treatment include the part of the mainsail which bears on the shrouds when running before the wind, and the foot of the genoa where it bears on the shrouds when close hauled. Patch in the same way as a tear, only this time you do not have to trim the sail and you thus avoid having to sew a second time from the other side. But you do have to put a second patch on the other side, and this one should be slightly larger than the first, so that you only have to sew through two thicknesses of cloth at any time. Here again, you should mark the work carefully in pencil, and take care to see that the warp and weft are lined up. As chafing pieces tend to be long and narrow, you will save a good deal of time if you put them on with a sewing machine, but you would be advised to add a few hand stitches at the corners, because the stouter twine will be better able to stand up to rough treatment.

Spinnakers

Spinnakers are only different to repair from fore and aft sails in that they call for more delicate work. You will be able to tackle most jobs with a domestic needle and thread, and almost any sewing machine can be used (even with a straight stitch) providing the sail is not so large that it cannot be passed under the arm of the machine.

Patches. Adhesive nylon repair tape makes an excellent job of mending tears in spinnakers, to last at least for a season. If you put a few stitches in the tape as well, there is no reason why the job should not be permanent. Any ordinary patch should have its edges turned under and not heat-sealed, so that the repair will be stronger, but a heat-sealed patch will hold if the stitching is zigzag and crosses the edge of the cloth to stop it fraying out.

Leeches. A common tear is one which runs down the leech just inside the tape. If it is a clean straight tear, you may be able to patch it with adhesive nylon tape and two rows of stitching. This sort of damage, however, is usually jagged and goes for at least half the sail, and the light cloth will almost certainly be frayed too much to sew straight back to the leech tape – with or without the help of repair tape. You have to take the leech tape off, from head to clew, trim the cloth clean in an even curve throughout its length, rub it down or heat-seal it to a new line 2 or 3 inches in from the original, and then replace the leech tape using a sewing machine. If any tape is left sewn to the untorn leech, you should strike it up with pencil match marks well into the sail before you take it off; this will be a guide to tension when you replace it later. If, however, you have managed to get the sail down quickly and the tear is not more than about 10 per cent of the length of the leech, you can try a patch. These long narrow repairs are not easy, but you will stand less risk of spoiling the set of the leech this way than you will by removing the tape altogether and rerubbing the leech as above. Cut the patch to size, taking it round the tape and back on the other side, so that it is doubled. Rub it down to crease it to shape, turn the hem under and pin it in place. Then machine at least two rows of stitching into the old cloth and one into the tape; put a few hand stitches at top and bottom so that the patch lies flat on the sail.

Chafe. As we saw in Chapter 4, chafe can attack the head, foot and clews. The foot must be tackled much as the leeches described above. The head and clews will need to be dealt with as they come, with patches and darns being put in as required; we shall see in the next chapter how to deal with eyes and cringles. If the head swivel is shackled to the sail, so that it is free to work from side to side and chafe the cloth, it is worth seeing whether a firm seizing will hold it steady and put a stop to it. If the sail tears just outside the reinforcing patch at head, tack or clew, undo the reinforcement next to the tear, patch well underneath it and sew it back on again.

Broken Wire. If examination by pulling the leeches out side by side shows that one is longer than the other, then one of the wires is broken and needs to be replaced or mended. This can be effected by adding an extra length to the existing wire by means of a Talurit or Nicopress swaging (using a double ferrule or collar). Locate the break by feel and unpick enough of the tape to expose the broken ends and get them on a swaging press. Clean up the break and join enough new wire to make the two leeches exactly the same length again; wrap any new swagings so that they do not chafe through the luff tape. Resew the tape.

Replacing the Wire. If the wire is weak in several places, or has broken so near to the head eye that a new length cannot be joined to the stub end, the whole wire should be replaced. This involves taking off the tape tabling and unpicking the head eye and both clew exit holes. A new wire of full length must be fitted with a loop at the head to form the ring which is hand worked as an eye, complete with liner in the normal way. Resew the leech tapes round the wire, fit new exit holes and form eyes at the lower ends of the two sides of the wire exactly the same as before. Tidy up.

Broken Tape. It is likely that this repair will be accompanied by a torn panel in the sail as well, because a broken tape will put all the strain on the nylon. If you are lucky enough to catch it before the tape has broken right through, it is merely a question of pat-

Plate 6. **Roping**. *The palm is still pushing, but the finger and thumb are already in position to grasp the needle as it comes out on the other side of the work.* Author.

ching the broken area with a new piece of tape wrapped round the leech on both sides. The length involved is usually short, and two or three inches of stitching are quickly put in by hand.

Roping

If a luff rope is hand sewn, its attachment to the sail is a specialist job but not necessarily one which need frighten the determined owner. In any event, the most likely repair is only going to be a short length which has pulled away and needs resewing.

The method is described in Appendix B. Get some practice before you start in earnest, and remember that the secret is to advance the needle a little *after* passing it through the rope, and *before* entering it into the sail. This is so that you sew the rope on with the extra sailcloth it needs if both are finally to stretch to the same length (because, if rope is not the prestretched variety, it stretches more than sailcloth). Use of a bench hook and match marks will help a lot.

If by any chance you need to reshape the sail to alter the draft in it (of which more anon), you will have to take the rope off altogether. Before doing this, strike it up with a pencil, by putting match marks across rope and sail at intervals of about 1 foot. In this

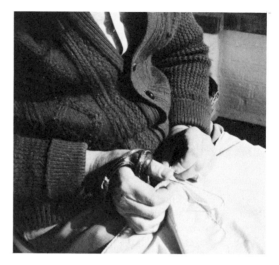

way you will be able to put it back on again with the same tension – but use a light pull on the stitches when resewing, or you will find that there is too little rope and too much sail.

Reroping. Use prestretched polyester rope (Terylene or Dacron) and you are not then bothered by having to put on less rope than sail, to allow for unequal stretch. Cut off enough rope to be sure of having 1 foot or so left over at the end (because it is better to have a foot too much than 4 inches too little, after all that work), shake all the twists out of it and run a pencil line down its length as a check that it doesn't twist while you are sewing. Stretch it out alongside the sail and pull both steady, then strike the two up at intervals of not more than 1 foot. If you only need to rerope because of a broken strand, you will be safer to unpick about a foot each side of the break and either lay in a new strand about two feet long or, if the other strands are weakened, join a short length by means of a long splice. It is better if the spliced in section is marginally shorter than the original, rather than longer, because the splice is sure to settle and elongate slightly. This will always be a weak point, but you stand less risk of deforming the sail this way.

Casing. The rope at the top of the luff and the outer end of the foot (head and clew) is subject to a lot of strain and movement, so it is often protected by leather or canvas casing. This must be taken off first, but put by for refitting later; you will recall that hide leather can be softened by soaking for half an hour or so in cold water.

Tape. Where a rope is fastened to a sail by being sewn to the outside of a length of tape, which in turn is sewn to the sail, it will be attached by machine stitching. Repair problems will usually be connected with the rope pulling away from the tape. The easiest way to sew it back is by hand, to the edge of the tape, so a sailmaker's palm is still your best bet. In any event, for machine sewing you have to have a special machine which can punch needles right through the rope. Treat it, therefore, exactly as if it were hand sewn in the first place, and accept the fact that it will lie against the tape at a slightly different angle. If the rope is encased inside the tape, and the latter has pulled away, it either needs sewing back on again or, if it is torn, patching; such a patch can be put on right round the rope only if it is not going to make it too bulky to run in the mast or boom groove.

Headboards

All this talk of roping brings us naturally to the mainsail's headboard. By its very nature, this is closely associated with the luff rope. A board on any mainsail which is attached to the mast by slides, is often an internal one with the luff rope continuing over the top and down the aft side. If it should break, the rope must be taken off to a point below the headboard, the top of the sail must be unstitched and the board removed from the pocket in the head of the sail (there may be some heavy external stitching through both board and sail as well). It will probably be of plastic or light alloy, and you should get another of the same size, slip it into the pocket and replace all the stitching you have just taken out. Headboards which are riveted on the outside of the sail do not affect the stitching of sail or rope, and can be attended to independently if you have the right equipment.

Chafe at the Head. If the rope is one which runs in a mast groove, it will end level with the top of the headboard, and the rope does not need removing to replace the board. But the trouble most likely to occur here is one of wear on the cloth between the headboard and the rope, where it chafes in the groove; this can reach a point where the cloth wears nearly through. The simplest repair is to add some body to the cloth by means of sewing back and forth with a stout twine, using long running stitches. The point to remember here is that the cloth is already weak and too many needle holes will weaken it further, so thread a quadruple twine on as small a needle as you can and try to pick some solid cloth to sew through. Run up and down about four times and then hammer flat and wax it. If the cloth is too badly torn for this repair to hold, take off the rope and patch the sail right round the luff on both sides; you may have to remove the headboard as well if you want to get the patch well into the sail on to firm cloth. Take care before you go too far that

the thicker result of your efforts will fit easily in the mast groove. If it is too tight a fit, it will only chafe more quickly than it already has done, and you should unpick the reinforcement patches at the head, take out the board and remove some of the defective cloth, before doing a bigger job altogether, in what is virtually a replacement of the head patches.

Two slides should be fitted to the headboard of any boat which cruises extensively or which is longer than about 35 feet overall. If you only have one slide on yours, add a second if the board has a suitable hole to take it.

Luff Wires

A metal luff wire usually gives way either at the tack splice (be it hand worked – not often found these days – or a Talurit or Nicopress crimped eye), or else in the bottom one or two feet of the wire. This is because the formation of the eye disturbs the plastic coating which often covers the wire, thus letting in salt water to cause oxydisation; secondly, the luff wire – be it stainless steel or plastic-coated galvanised – is subject to most strain in this area, and flexing coupled with tension can cause individual strands to break and weaken the whole construction.

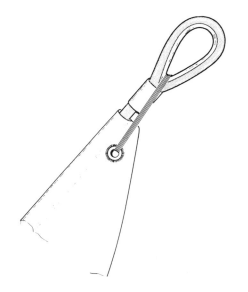

18. **Jib Eye (Wire).** *The small eyelet at the head of the luff tabling is used to pull the sail along the wire and induce draft. It is then seized to the head eye and covered with a small sailcloth casing (not shown).*

Replacement of a luff wire is a major repair. It entails carefully cutting out the old wire, making up a new one to exactly the same length and fitting it to the sail. Although this is not particularly difficult, it sounds easier than it is. Try to pull a length of cord through the tabling when you remove the old wire, for this is easier than unpicking the stitching all down the luff; in either case

the eyelets will probably have to be removed. Make up the new wire, pull it through or sew it into the tabling, and work the tack eye into the sail as before, taking care to pick up all the several thicknesses of cloth in the area. The thimble should be stainless or bronze for stainless steel wire, and nylon for galvanised wire; the swaging ferrules should be copper and light alloy respectively (to avoid galvanic corrosion).

Set up the wire horizontally as if checking out a headsail for draft or fault examination. There will be a small eyelet at the head of the luff tabling. Tie a length of stout twine (for a dinghy) or cord (for a cruising boat) to this eyelet, pass it through the head eye and pull the sail vigorously along the wire to induce draft up the luff. The amount of pull varies with the size of sail and weight of canvas, and it can be as little as 2 inches or as much as 1 foot; a broad generalisation is to pull 1 inch for every 3 feet of sail luff. Take the twine or cord back and forth between the eyelet and the head eye and tie off securely (fig. 18). Replace the sailcloth or leather casing which will have covered this lashing.

Run a row of tacking stitches along the tabling hard up against the wire to hold it well forward and, if you have had to remove the luff eyelets (which is highly likely), you are in for a long session of getting practice at punching or hand sewing them back again.

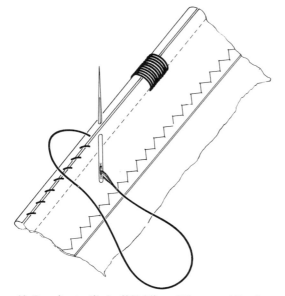

19. **Repairs to Jib Luff Tabling**. *Where a tabling has been cut off and sewn back again, as opposed to being rolled over, there will be a row of vulnerable stitching along the extreme front edge of the sail. The round stitch is used when strengthening is needed; take care not to puncture any plastic coating on the wire.*

Finally, seize the luff firmly round the wire at intervals and the job is complete.

Stitching. Some headsails are made with the tabling merely rolled on itself, others have the tabling cut off when the sail is made and moved across to be refitted so that the threadlines run parallel to each other instead of across the grain. Where this has been done, there will be a row of stitching right up the very front of the wire, and this can get weakened. Strength is put back to the sail by hand work involving the round stitch, laboriously taken the full length of any weak places. Take care not to put the needle through any plastic coating which is over the wire or you will let water into it. Stitches should be kept small and well spaced (to avoid perforating the weakened cloth too much) and don't worry too much if you don't catch both cloths every now and then; the strength of the job will not be impaired by the odd missed stitch (fig. 19).

six

Repairs to Sail Accessories

Sails have a wide range of accessories, all of which need renewing or repairing from time to time. When they need attention it is normally fairly obvious, so we need not waste any time discussing how and where to identify the problems. They will tell you soon enough themselves.

Eyes

The head, tack and clew eyes of a sail are subjected to particularly heavy loadings. The mainsail head eye is usually incorporated in the headboard and, if it is worn through or broken, it will require replacement of the board as we have just seen in Chapter 5. Hand-sewn tack and clew eyes often start to show wear by distortion of the brass turn-over or liner which is punched in to prevent chafe on the stitching. You may not have the right size liner to put in a new one (it also needs the correct size punch and die to do the job) but, if you are lucky enough to catch the problem early, you may be able to beat it out again with a hammer and spike.

If the eye is distorted into an oval shape, it is almost certain that the brass ring which is sewn into the sail first, is broken. This may not show, but the strength of the eye has completely gone and it must come out for a new ring to be sewn in, together with

protecting liner. This can be the same size as the original only if the cloth is not also torn. In this event you may be able to put in a bigger eye, which will enable you to sew into good cloth, or you may have to fit a patch first. In the latter case, take off the rope for 4 or 5 inches round the eye, run the patch round both sides of the sail, resew the rope and then work a new eye close up to the rope.

Where a distorted eye is a punched fitting, possibly with a steel liner rather than a brass one, you will have to break it away from the sail and work a new ring as above. It may have failed in the first place because it was punched and not sewn (brass eyes are weaker than steel ones in this respect), so you will produce a stronger job if you hand sew.

If the stitching shows signs of strain immediately next to a tack or clew eye, this is the result of the high loadings put on the sail from these points. Take out the brass turn-over and fit a foot or so of $\frac{1}{2}$–1 inch wide webbing tape (or heavy sailcloth with sealed edges) through the eye and then along each side of the sail in the direction of the strain; this will help spread the load. Use wide stitches, well spaced as in fig. 20. If you have no replacement turnover, leave it in and fit the webbing over the top of it, taking care to keep clear of the bearing surface of the eye to avoid chafe by shackles etc. This is also a useful reinforcement for leech cringles.

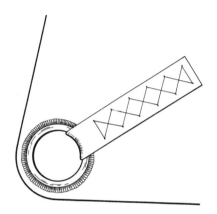

20. **Webbing Reinforcement.** *Large stitches criss-cross the webbing to avoid too much perforation of an already strained cloth; the tape may go over or under the metal liner of the eye, providing the bearing surface is left clear.*

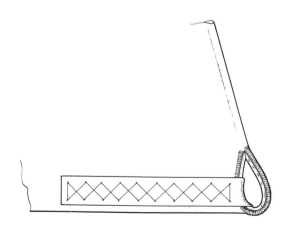

Cunningham Hole. If your sail has no Cunningham hole, fitting one is one of the best jobs for the amateur to tackle. You will be working on undamaged cloth and, if the result is a failure for any reason (perish the thought), it need not be used and thus will not be subjected to any strain. Indeed you (or your sailmaker) can always fit another just above the wreck of the first. It is a straight-forward hand-sewn eye worked into the luff, close to the rope if the sail has slides, or with enough room for a groove if necessary. It should go about 3 per cent of the luff length above the tack; say 6 to 7 inches on the average dinghy and up to 12 to 18 inches as the sail gets bigger.

Reef Points. A torn reef point must receive high priority for repair, because it is only used in heavy weather and you never know when you are going to need it. If just the small eyelet has gone, its replacement is as described above: unpick it and work in a new one by hand. If the sail itself is torn, you must put on a patch. Remove the eyelet and then take off the small strengthening patches (probably diamond-shaped) from each side of the sail. Put on a repair patch in the usual way, taking special care to see that you cover any part of the sail which may have been weakened by the tear. Replace the patches, work a new eyelet (it may have to be bigger than the original if you are restricted in the spares and gear you have) and then refit the reef point if appropriate.

Slides

The traditional method of attaching slides is with waxed twine, and this has served well for many years. Its chief drawback is chafe, for only one part of the seizing has to break for the whole thing to be in danger of coming undone.

Various methods of overcoming this have been tried, one being to use a thimble to take the chafe at the slide. Sometimes a shackle is preferred, but this means that the slide is a little bit slacker on the sail, and thus more prone to twist and jam on the track. Shackles also chafe the luff rope heavily, which has to be well protected in way of every slide by means of hide or cloth casing, or else by special plastic liners (fig. 21). The two advantages of the shackle are strength, and the fact that it can be quickly and easily fitted by the owner. The disadvantages, however, make a formidable list which more than outweigh the points in favour.

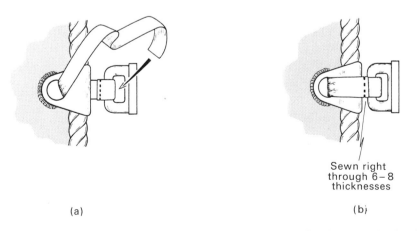

Sewn right
through 6−8
thicknesses

(a)   (b)

21. **Taped Slides.** *Synthetic tape is strong and resists chafe, yet remains flexible. Protection for the rope is not essential, but it should ideally be cased with sailcloth or, as here, with a plastic liner.*

1. The shackle itself can corrode, so that the pin will not undo. Electrolysis between shackle and slide often accelerates this.

2. The shackle will chafe the boltrope, which has to be cased with leather or cloth as some measure of protection.

3. The softer of the two metals will chafe, either on the slide or on the shackle.

4. There is extra weight aloft.

5. If an odd-sized shackle has to be used for one or two slides, the boltrope will not run in a straight line.

Which brings me to what the solution is. To my mind the answer is to attach the slides by means of Terylene or Dacron tape. This type of tape is strong enough to resist chafe by the slide, and is soft enough not to chafe the slide or sail in return.

One end of about 1 foot of $\frac{1}{2}$-inch tape is first sewn to the slide. The other end is then passed through the eyelet at the luff or foot, and then back through the slide. This is repeated as many times as will conveniently go, usually about three or four times to give six or eight parts. Care should be taken to see that a slight amount of lateral play is allowed the slide, so that the sail can swing from side to side on the mast. The loose end should then be sewn through the six or eight parts several times with a stout synthetic twine. The result is a neat and workmanlike fitting which will last a good deal longer than most other systems, and one which will not damage the slide or the sail (fig. 21).

Another method, somewhat on the same lines, is to use a leather thong or strap. Either soften it well by soaking it in water and sew as if it were tape, or else cut a slit in one end, pass the other end two or three times through both slide and eyelet, and then through the slit; finish the job off with a half hitch.

There are, however, slides which do not have a wide enough handle to take a tape. More often than not these are the external claw type which, besides being narrow at this point, also tend to be made of thin enough metal to cut twine, thread or, indeed, tape; they normally have a brass thimble for a grommet or seizing, but this makes them slack on the sail.

If for any reason you cannot put on tape, a seizing can be made to spread the load on the handle of the slide by separating the turns into two parts, ensuring that one part is laid round one end of the handle and the second part is round the other end. They can be kept at their respective ends by taking the cross turns round the two parts in a figure-of-eight pattern, with the crossover separating the two seizings.

Some people find that these seizings are more easily put on with the help of a needle.

Hanks or Snap Hooks

Dinghies have a wide variety of hanks and snap hooks from which to choose. Besides the end- and side-pull piston type, of either bronze or stainless steel, there are wire clips like overgrown safety pins, nylon and metal twist-type attachments (known sometimes as Badger slides), and tab hanks; zippers also come under this heading.

Wire clips will not stand up to the heaviest weather without tending to bend, nylon twist hanks chafe on the forestay, metal Badger slides are sometimes hard to get off with cold fingers, and gunmetal or stainless piston hanks are not everyone's idea of perfection. Tab hanks can be put on by the amateur, so I will describe them for those who would like to give them a try.

A short piece of synthetic webbing, about 1¼ inches wide, is sewn to the luff of the headsail so that it protrudes some 1½ inches beyond the luff. This is passed round the forestay and fastened to itself by means of a press-stud (fig. 22). Its advantages are lightness, minimal disturbance of the airflow and unlikelihood of its catching on the spinnaker. Disadvantages are chafe of the tab on the forestay, and the undue reliance which has to be placed on the fastener, which may not always be corrosion free – particularly as regards its spring.

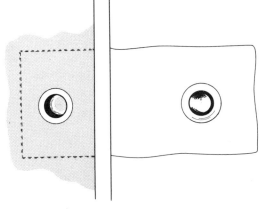

*22. **Tab Hank**. This is an economical and light way of attaching the jib to the forestay on smaller boats. It wears rather easily and the press studs tend to corrode, but it is quickly replaced if necessary.*

Most hanks and snap hooks are attached to the sail with a seizing or else, in the smaller sizes, they are squeezed on to the luff by means of crimping special arms on to the eyelets. Other systems include screws, pins, and leather thongs.

Where hanks or snap hooks are seized by twine, use of a needle makes the operation much easier, as with slides. Often a few turns can be put on over an existing seizing, but take care not to hide a basically weak attachment. If this is the case, remove all the old seizing and start from zero again. Anchor a

Plate 7. **Oiling.** *Don't put more than one or two drops of oil on the moving parts of piston hanks or snap hooks, or it will spread to the sail and be unsightly.* Author.

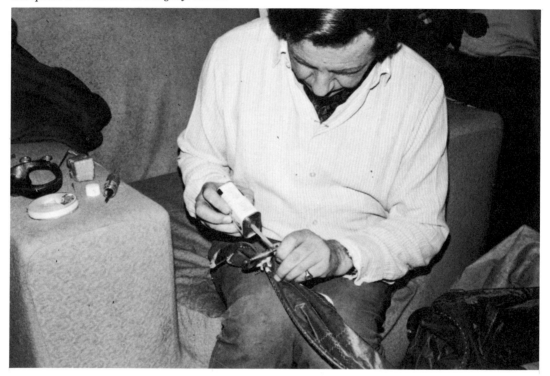

heavy doubled twine on one loop of the hank or hook, and place the latter against the eyelet so that the spring plunger or piston lies in the same sense as those on the rest of the sail. The twine is then passed back and forth through the eyelet and through the two loops on the hank or hook. When you have done this a dozen times or so, alternate with turns taken through the loops but *outside* the luff

wire. The job is finally finished off by taking cross turns round the whole seizing to bind it together.

In the case of hanks or snap hooks which are fastened to headsails by screwing through the sail or by means of squeezing metal jaws together, refitting is a question of carefully examining the item to make sure that it neither has a worn thread nor is fatigued;

replacement is almost more of a job for a garage mechanic than a sailmaker. Put two drops of oil on any spring plunger which is sticking (not more, to prevent it dripping on to the sail itself).

Windows

It is easier to fit a window in a jib than in a mainsail, because this sail lies flatter and is smaller and easier to handle on the machine. Before you start, look up your class rules if you have any, in case they have restrictions as to size and position of such an item. Even if you do not race the boat yourself, you should keep within the rule, so that you do not spoil the sail's value for any subsequent buyer of your boat. It is worth settling for a window 2 or 3 inches less in size all round so that, in the event of your efforts being unsuccessful, you can ask your sailmaker to fit one to cover your mistake; he will almost certainly have to cut away extra cloth to true up the job.

Being made of a material which bends but does not distort or stretch (you will probably have to buy it from your sailmaker), a window should be placed in a fairly flat part of the sail, otherwise it will have to try to take up complex multiple curves and will thus make creases. It should be sewn on to the sail before the opening is cut, so that it lies evenly over the area and does not pull at one corner.

A professional may fit a patch slightly larger than the window first, leaving one end open as a sort of envelope into which the window is fitted. The opening is then closed and the window sewn in. He then cuts away the cloth from both sides, leaving enough to turn $\frac{1}{2}$-inch hems under, and sews round again. In this way the sharp edge of the window is covered on both sides. But this is time consuming and difficult, so we shall sew the window straight on to the sail.

Mark the position by drawing carefully round the window (it should have radiused corners, so that the sewing machine can go round them easily, and so that they do not stick out sharply). Lay the window on the sail, using double-sided sticky tape to keep it in place, and then sew round. If you are using a zigzag stitch, the first row should be right at the edge so that the stitching goes partly on and partly off the window material, but a straight stitch is acceptable, for it will not have to move with the cloth (there is no stretch in the window).

Now turn the sail over, cut out the opening on the other side, leaving enough to turn under, then crease this hem by rubbing down. Sew round again and the job is done (fig. 23). If you use a delicate touch, it is possible to cut away the opening with a soldering iron or

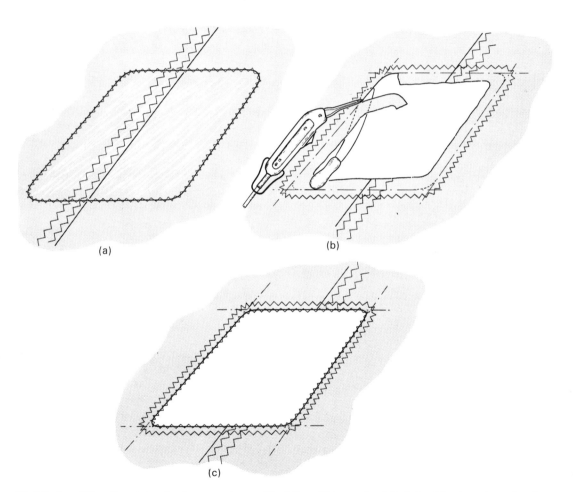

23. **Window.** *When the window has been sewn to one side of the sail (a), rough cut the hole with scissors from the other side. Trim round with a soldering iron, using a palette knife as backing (b). Sew the edge down and the job is complete (c).*

heated knife, but you obviously have to take great care not to burn the window itself; once you have made a start, you can slip a metal blade (ruler, or pastry knife from the kitchen) into the opening as a protection while cutting. This will avoid having to turn the edge of the sail under, and is thus an easier sewing job.

Battens

Wooden battens are liable to split, particularly at the inner end, which is often tapered to allow it to bend enough. A solution to this problem lies in prevention rather than cure: bind the end with adhesive tape before the split ever occurs.

One other frequent fault with battens is that they are sometimes a quarter of an inch too long for their pockets. If the batten has to be forced hard to get it into the sail, you should take time out to trim a little off the length. Tackle the thicker end as it is easier to cut without splitting it, and you also do not want to remove any of the flexibility. Make sure to smooth over all corners and rough edges.

Full-length battens will have some kind of protectors or antichafe pads fitted on the outside of the pocket, where the end bears against the mast. These may be no more than 2 or 3 inches of rope sewn on each side of the luff so that they lie snug against the mast when the sail is hoisted. Or they may be leather pads or proprietary specialist items made of nylon or other plastic. These should be checked for security or, indeed, added if not already fitted.

Leechlines

I do not necessarily suggest that you should attempt to fit a leechline to a sail which does not already have one. The leech tabling would almost certainly not present a continuous run for such an insertion, and you would probably have to unpick and resew so many seams that damage to the set of the sail would be inevitable. This would merely serve to add to your leech problems rather than provide you with a cure. But a leechline can break, and replacement is not difficult.

The line either starts at the aft edge of the headboard, on the outside of the sail, and is then led into the tabling through a small eyelet two or three inches from the starting point, or it is started right inside the tabling altogether. At all events you have to find the source, even if it means unpicking a short length of seam or tabling to get at it.

Remove the remains of the old leechline

and prepare a sufficient length of new line; don't use anything thicker than the original, because weight at the leech can cause vibration of the sail. Now may be the time to fit a leechline long enough to carry from the clew along the boom to the tack, so that you can reach it for adjustment on all points of sailing. Sew the upper end to the aft face of the headboard. (On larger craft in the old days, where the luff rope was carried round the board and tapered in a rat's tail at its aft edge, a professional would have spliced the end of a laid line, as opposed to braided, to the taper of the boltrope. But this is rarely done these days.) Attach the other end to a straight piece of wire, about 8 inches long, by sewing through the line and half-hitching it to the wire; a nick cut in the wire will help it hold. Then feed the wire through the eyelet at the head of the sail and work it hand over hand down the tabling. There will be an exit eyelet at the bottom of the tabling, either just above the clew or else, on a sail fitted with reef points or eyelets, just above the reef cringle at the leech. Bring the wire and leechline through this exit eyelet and cut off as required.

If you propose carrying the line forward to the tack, you should sew one or two small brass rings or hoops to the footrope or foot tabling to act as fairleads.

The exit hole is usually nothing more than a punched eyelet, and this can sometimes pull away under the action of a stressed leechline. It is, of course, punched into one side of the tabling only (if it were right through both sides, how could the leechline get out?). If you cannot persuade the liner back into place securely, you have to open up the tabling at this point, remove the leechline from the exit hole, and punch in a new eyelet – often slightly larger than the original so that any damaged cloth can be properly caught between the two halves of the eyelet.

If it is badly torn, the tabling may have to be patched first, but you are by now enough of an old hand to undertake a little job like that. In this case it will be easier to open up the tabling 3 or 4 inches higher up the leech than the original exit hole, pull out the leechline and pick out the remains of the old eyelet. Fit a new eyelet 3 or 4 inches above the old one, reeve the leechline through it and then patch over the old eyelet right round both sides of the sail, without having to bother about leaving the tabling free for the passage of the line; you can then carry on stitching to resew the tabling opposite the new exit hole.

Leechline Buttons. Fastening off a leechline is often a cumbersome process involving further eyelets in the sail, which in turn means knotting the end of the line. Since the

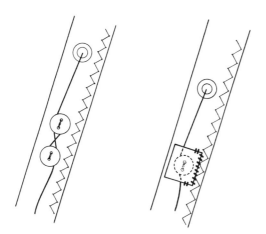

24. **Leechline Buttons.** *One or two small leather buttons make tying off the leechline much easier. A small cover is needed on any sail which is liable to chafe its clew on shrouds or mast.*

early 1960s I have advocated use of a button at the lower end of the leech, which can be used as a cleat (see my book *Sails*). The simplest form of this is a plastic button from the sewing box, but this is liable to break, so leather or rubber is better. Large sails may need two buttons, one above the other, so that a line may be fastened off in figure-of-eight fashion. This works well on mainsails, but headsails need a small flap to cover the buttons, so that they do not snag on shrouds or tear off on the mast as the boat tacks.

The flap should be moderately stiff canvas and sewn along its forward edge only (fig. 24).

Tell-Tales

Tell-tales, wind tallies or streamers – call them what you will – sewn into the genoa (and other sails) are quickly got used to, easy to work with and give an excellent idea of what is happening to the flow of air over the sail at important points. Aerodynamics are outside the scope of this book but I cannot resist reminding you that it is laminar flow you are seeking, particularly to windward, and tell-tales reveal this desirable state of affairs. You turn away from a lifting streamer or you sheet the sail towards it.

Select a 1-foot length of wool, nylon thread or narrow (under $\frac{1}{4}$ inch) spinnaker cloth which contrasts with your sails (dark for white sails and white for tan, red or blue ones) and sew it into the luff of the genoa at quarter, half and three-quarter heights; strips of cloth can be glued or fastened with sticky tape. The idea is to have 6 inches hanging free on each side, and you should take a round stitch with a half hitch as you go, in order to anchor the thread firmly. The exact positioning of the tell-tale is not particularly important, except that it should be within 9–12 inches of the luff to give the best answers, and more than 6 inches from any seam or the luff so that it does not get snagged while in use. It should also, of course, be where it can be seen easily by the helmsman.

A dark tell-tale can be seen through most white jibs, so that you will be able to follow both windward and leeward indications.

Roller Boom Vang

When a mainsail is rolled round its boom in a reef, there is no way of attaching a boom vang or kicking strap directly to the boom, because the sail is covering the attachment points. It is possible to use a claw arrangement but this is clumsy and, in any case, does not offer the sewing practice presented by the strap system. Dinghies, day sailers, cruisers and offshore racers can all use this with advantage.

Select a length of suitable webbing (2–5 in wide and 3–6 ft long) and cut it off by heat-sealing both ends. Now work a stout eye by hand near to one end, and the job is done. The free end of the strap is rolled in with the last few rolls of the mainsail, to leave the eye hanging down as an anchorage point for a vang.

Zippers

You are not likely to have to fit a zipper from scratch, because a sail has to be cut with this in mind when it is made (either to have extra fullness along the foot if it is a mainsail, or else to have a flap to wrap round the forestay if it is a jib). You may, however, want to remove an old zipper which does not work, in order to fit a new one. Choose one with the teeth made of synthetic material and with a well-protected metal slider; not every zipper adapts itself to sailing, and it is important to check that you have the right make. It is a good idea to have a second slider permanently on a mainsail zipper, ready to be brought into use if the first one breaks.

Mark the line of the faulty zipper before you take it off. Lay the new one on the sail and strike up both halves, checking across at frequent intervals to see that the two parts of the sail are going to lie happily together when the zip is closed, without one pulling aft or forward on the other. This matching of the halves is an important step.

Now sew the zip on by machine, using two rows along each half, and taking care not to sew too close to the teeth, nor indeed too far away (check on the original to see the right distance). Put a few hand stitches at each end and – on mainsails only – sew right round the two sets of teeth which are permanently closed, to hold them tightly together and to act as a stop when the slider is in the open position. If you have a spare slider, see that it is at this end, and sew the teeth together on both sides of the slider. If it has to be brought into use, one lot of hand stitching is cut away and the second slider can then move up the teeth closing them as it goes; there will still be a set of strengthening stitches at the very end of the teeth.

seven

Examining for Faulty Set

Before examining ways in which to correct various faults in sails, we should look at the whole question of how to identify and isolate a fault. In this way we can not only clear our own minds as to the problem and whether it is curable at home but also, if it is going to be a job for the professional, we can pinpoint the symptoms so that the sailmaker has the best information we can give him, in case he cannot check for himself by going out sailing with you for any reason. It will be safest in this identifying process to assume from the start that you are going to need the pro's help in curing any faults; in this way you should not only be able to assess whether you can do the job yourself but, should you find that the task is beyond your own resources, you will have covered all the ground and got all the answers which the sailmaker will need.

An indoor (horizontal) or outdoor (vertical) test rig is a useful adjunct to a sailmaker's armoury in the fight against creases and bad shape, and he will almost certainly set up in his loft any suspect sails brought in for cure, unless the problem is obvious. A test rig, however, cannot always reproduce the conditions found afloat, particularly if it is a horizontal one, and it serves best in conjunction with observation of the offending sail on its own spars under sailing conditions. A rig enables closer examination of individual parts of the sail in order to confirm a condition found afloat. Let us therefore see how you can help the sailmaker with photographs, drawings and notes of any badly setting sail; this evidence will also, of course, be invaluable if you decide to try your hand at the cure at home.

Documentation

Take plenty of notes and measurements while afloat, and do not rely on your memory to write it all up afterwards. Secondly, mark the sail itself in pencil to help identify creases etc. Count seams or other reference points for creases out of reach of your pencil, and write it all down as you note distances (fig. 25).

Photographs. Black and white prints are best, but anything will do, transparencies or even movies (providing the sailmaker has got time to watch them), although the latter do not give a lasting image which can be placed under a magnifying glass for close examination. Plenty of contrast is what is needed, so make maximum use of shadows to highlight creases. Each sail should be photographed individually from leeward, if possible, as well as from windward. Those taken from windward should ideally be from the middle of the foot, pointing straight up the sail, trying to

Plate 8. **Test Masts.** *A sailmaker will usually have test spars for checking sails. Ratsey and Lapthorn can set cruiser, day boat and dinghy sails on this comprehensive rig. Beken.*

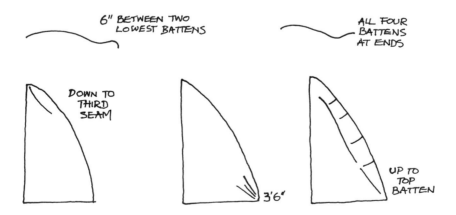

25. **Notes Taken Afloat on Faults.** *Anything written down while actually sailing is likely to be more accurate than your memory later. Sketches can complement photographs and pencil marks on the sail.*

Plate 9. **Indoor Test Rig.** *Like most sailmakers, Bruce Banks Sails have an indoor rig set horizontally. This dinghy mainsail can be looked at closely all round on a bendy mast as it takes up its natural camber under the influence of gravity.* Yachting World.

get as much of the upper half as possible into a close-up picture. For an effective general shot, try one from another boat (perhaps the dinghy) or from on shore – but keep in mind it is detail that is wanted, not background, so get close. Write down your shots as you take them because, if you are taking several, you will be surprised how hard it will be to identify a particular headsail if you have really got a close-up.

Notes. Take sketches, with measurements, while afloat, as shown in fig. 25. Make a note of the wind and other relevant information

26. **Headboard Pulled Over.** *If you cannot fit a larger sheave, a hard metal spacer can be added to the aft face of the mast to do two jobs: it will stop the sail going above the upper black band, and it will also force the halyard away from the mast so that it arrives at the headboard with a fair lead.*

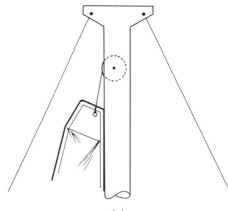

(a)

such as the sea state or sheeting conditions. Finally, list fully all the faults you find and then take your documentation to the sail-maker for discussion while it is still fresh in your memory.

Tune and Trim

Before going any further, let us see how the sailmaker goes about the job. A surprising number of creases can be traced to faulty tune or trim. It should go without saying that the mast must be straight on *both* tacks, and the rigging set up properly – sight up the luff of the mainsail for both lateral and fore and aft alignment, check on forestay sag from beside the stay. A mainsail made for a bendy mast should not be expected to set properly on a straight one and, more important, vice versa. See that all leechlines are completely slack, even where they may only have been steadied to quieten a gentle drumming, or else a false impression will be obtained. Now check that the sail in question has been bent on properly; this includes the following points.

Mainsail Luff. The sail should lead fairly to the tack pin. If this is set back from the mast to accommodate a bulky roller reefing gear, the sail must be cut accordingly or else

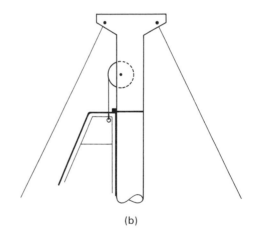

(b)

creases will show. Similarly, the halyard should lead straight down from the sheave to its attachment point at the headboard, and should not pull over towards the mast when the sail is fully hoisted (fig. 26).

Mainsail Slides. All slides should be at an even distance from the rope or tape. If an odd-sized shackle, or a slacker or tighter seizing has been used here and there, the luff will be out of alignment and creases will run from the offending points.

Mainsail Clew. The clew should be in a straight horizontal line with the rest of the foot. If it is allowed to rise, either because there is no slide at the clew eye, or because

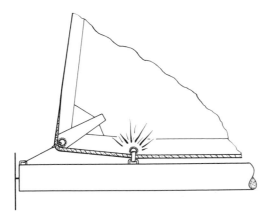

27. Mainsail Clew. *If you don't have a positive clew slide which holds the sail firmly down to the boom in metal jaws, fit a slide at the clew eye or take a lashing round the boom. The latter should also be done with a sail which runs in a groove, because high sheet loadings can cause the sail to pull out of the groove at the clew.*

there is no lashing round the boom at the clew, bad creases will result (fig. 27).

Battens. Battens should be of correct length for the pocket in question (you wouldn't smile if you had seen as many as I have which were quarter of an inch too long) and sufficiently flexible, particularly the top one.

Main Halyard Tension. A mainsail which is not hoisted hard enough will show a slack leech, precisely because the leech is slack. Haul the sail up properly and greater tension will be put on both luff *and* leech. See that any topping lift is slack.

Jib Sheet Fairlead. If the fairlead is too far forward, the leech will be tight and the foot slack; vice versa if it is too far aft. There may be reasons for this sort of situation, but normally the pull of the sheet should be divided between leech and foot so that the luff lifts evenly all along its length as the boat points above a close-hauled course.

Jib Luff. The luff should be in a straight line. The most usual trouble comes near the tack; either the tack itself is set back too far from the forestay, or else there is no hank or snaphook near the tack and this allows the luff to fall aft from the first hank or hook downwards, particularly if the sail is set on a tack pendant (fig. 28).

Jib Sag. If the forestay sags to leeward, the sail will become too full. There will not necessarily be any creases, but you will find yourself complaining rather vaguely that the boat will not point as well as your rivals.

Jib Hanks or Snap hooks. The points to watch here are somewhat similar to those regarding mainsail slides. A jib will suffer most, however, from hanks or snap hooks which are seized, and not screwed or squeezed on to the sail. If they have been lashed too tightly, thus compressing the eyelet and the cloth hard against the luff wire or rope, local creases will radiate from the seizing and there will tend to be a bigger crease running at right angles to the luff from this point.

Checks Afloat

You may think that some of the above is being rather particular. Let me remind you of the case of *Blue Leopard*. This large ketch was built in Britain and had, among others, a full suit of sails from the United States. A number of these sails appeared unsatisfactory to the experts during trials off Cowes, and

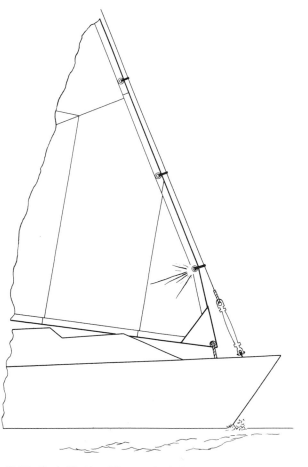

28. **Jib Tack Fitting**. *The cure is obvious in this particular case: see that the tack fitting is nearer the forestay; or fit a short tack strop and a hank or snap hook right at the tack.*

this was duly reported across the Atlantic. The American sailmaker concerned cabled the reply that he would fly over and do trials on the boat himself. If the owners were not then entirely satisfied, he would rectify the faults and pay his own fare. If, on the other hand, he could set the sails to their satisfaction, they would pay all his expenses. This was agreed.

At the end of the second lot of trials, the sailmaker was not a penny out of pocket and not a stitch had been altered in the sails.

Do not be tempted to sit at the marina berth or mooring and hoist only the sail you want to criticise. To get the right conditions you have to be sailing with the main and jib, because these two sails are both mutually supporting and mutually interfering, so you will never get a true picture of the one without the other.

Slack Leech. If the sail is a mainsail (or, to a lesser extent, if you are dealing with a rope luff jib), first check that the halyard is tight enough as has already been suggested above. Don't be restricted in this exercise by any black bands painted on the mast and boom, but pull the sail beyond the marks if you need to check the set at greater tension. If it looks better, then the sail will have to be shortened if it is required to stay within the rule; a cruising boat is not bothered by such petty

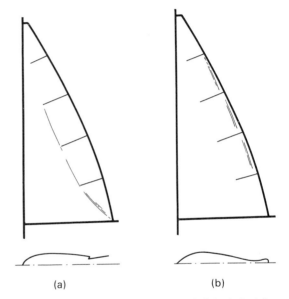

(a)   (b)

29. **Slack Mainsail Leech.** *A leech which is slack right into the sail for a good way, will reveal itself by a crease running along the ends of the battens as in (a). The inner ends of the battens tend to poke up to windward and the sail falls away to leeward from there out to the leech.*

If the last 3 or 4 inches only are slack as in (b), it is possible that the leech may vibrate in the wind. The sail may be perfectly all right aerodynamically, but the noise may get on the helmsman's nerves, so attend to it.

restrictions. If there are stops to prevent the sail going outside the marks and you want more luff tension, pull down on the Cunningham hole or, if one is not fitted, use the lowest slide eyelet instead. Next, try the leechline to see what effect it has on slackness. *Write down your findings.* In all probability a seam or seams will have to be tightened, so you should note the vertical and horizontal extent of the slackness, also if the tabling at the leech is slack, or whether it returns to tightness, to form a 'question mark' or cup when viewed from above or below (fig. 29).

Tight Leech. This is worse than a slack leech, because it means that the wind is not escaping from the sail properly. Double check the leechline, and then sight up the leech to discern the extent of the tightness: whether it extends into the sail, or stems purely from a tight leech tabling. The *appearance* of this fault can emanate from extreme fullness in a sail; it can also be caused in a jib by past misuse of the sail in winds too strong for the weight of cloth in question. As I said in Chapter 1 (and it will bear repeating several times), this is something from which most ghosters and light genoas suffer at one time or another, when the owner is reluctant to change to a heavier sail as the wind increases; the draft is then blown towards the leech as the cloth overstretches. A genuinely tight leech can be helped either by easing one or two seams and/or the tabling itself, or else by stretching the jib harder on its luff wire to draw the draft forward again.

Clew Creases. It is not possible within the scope of this chapter to list all sail creases and possible cures; I shall deal here with the most frequently met troubles of this kind. Multiple creases radiating from the clew probably come from tight sewing of the clew eye, coupled with the large stresses set up in the sail by modern winches and outhauls. They are hard to remove, but can sometimes be helped by a piece of stiffer cloth placed under the clew reinforcement, if the rules will allow it. One single crease running from a mainsail clew to the inner end of the lowest batten can result from a bad batten, a slack leech, a tight leech, too much roach, too much foot round (or fullness) at the clew, or overstretched cloth caused by badly laid panels or use of too light or poor quality sailcloth. So you can see that this is a difficult fault to diagnose and all the information you can produce, backed by photographs, is essential. Even then I do not hold out too much hope of the sailmaker being able to pronounce a verdict with any confidence, unless he goes out in the boat. If a boat has a bendy mast, a crease which runs from the clew to halfway up the luff somewhere near the point of maximum mast bend almost certainly means that the sail is not right for the mast. There has to be a lot of round to the luff of any mainsail made for a mast which is going to bow forward, thus taking up a good deal of slack cloth. If the sail

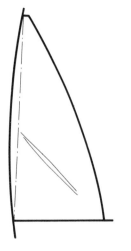

30. **Clew Creases.** *A bendy mast has to be properly matched with its sail. The crease above betrays the fact that this particular sail has not got enough luff round for the flexibility of its mast.*

does not have the cloth, the mast will pull a crease down to the clew (fig. 30).

Rope Creases. Small creases running at an angle from the boltrope of a mainsail or jib indicate either that the sail needs hauling up or out more, or else show that it is rope-bound – which means that too little rope has been put on to the sail, which therefore cannot be stretched properly due to the limitation of the length of rope. If it will go, try

pulling the sail beyond the black band to see the effect, and then measure the amount of sail that needs to be cut off; if the sail will not pull out, you will have to assess the extra amount it needs to be stretched – which is not a job for the inexperienced.

Batten Creases. A crease along the inner ends of the battens may mean that there is too much roach to be properly supported by the battens: about one-third of the batten length can safely be set outside the line from head to clew. Roach can be measured and the excess trimmed off. Otherwise this fault could result from a generally slack leech. In this case, double check that the main halyard is hard up (if it is, and the headboard can rise no higher, pull down on the lowest slide eyelet and the outer end of the boom at the same time, to simulate a tighter halyard), then take action as described above under Slack Leech.

Headboard Creases. These may stem from the stitching round the headboard being too tight. Alternatively, the halyard may be pulling the board over towards the mast when the sail is right up, either because the lead is not vertical from the sheave, or else because there should be another slide near the top of the headboard – possibly a combination of both.

Sail Too Full. Before deciding that a mainsail is too full, check the jib leech to see that it is not curling and backwinding the luff of the mainsail thus giving an impression of overfullness to the latter; this can also occur if the slot is too narrow. If a sail is genuinely too full, it is easy to flatten it along the luff by pleating; a sailmaker will want to know how far up the luff to continue the pleat, and roughly how much fullness should be taken out – an estimation which requires experience. If it is decided later that the correction was wrong, it is equally easy to rip the stitching and restore the sail to its original condition, save for two rows of stitch holes which will cause no harm.

Sail Too Flat. A mainsail which is too flat will need major surgery and should be seen by a sailmaker when it is set on spars. It is rare for a jib to be too flat, because it should be flatter than a mainsail anyway, and also it can be given more draft by easing the sheet. One of the few cases which occurs in jibs at all regularly is for part of the sail to be flat at the luff, while part is too full. As I said earlier, it may be that the luff has moved on the wire. This movement will first be manifested by small girts running from the hanks or snap hooks at an acute angle to the wire (this angle helps to distinguish this fault from hanks or snaps which have been seized too tightly,

which are revealed by radial creases nearly at right angles), and will later show as localised flat and full spots if the fault is not corrected as described in Chapter 8.

Spinnakers. Spinnakers suffer from three main faults. First, they may be too full for anything other than a dead run. This is a matter of how much cloth has been put into the head, and a photograph of the sail is really necessary if you are going to get a sailmaker to deal with it, although he can get a good idea by spreading the sail on his floor folded in half down the middle. Secondly, it may have two girts running from the head towards the middle of the sail, one each side of the vertical. These either stem from the sail being too full in the head or else from incorrectly gauged broad seam; take a photograph from behind the sail on the foredeck. The last of the more common faults is one of tight leeches. These make the sides of the sail curl in and are often caused by the tapes which are sewn along the edge being too short – either from shrinkage or from being put on tight in the first place. You should note how much the sail curls and to what degree, so that the sailmaker can estimate how the tapes should be eased. I have not listed the most common spinnaker fault of all: too narrow in the head compared with others in your class. The cure here is to go and take a look from somebody

Plate 10. **Your Own Test Rig**. *This dinghy jib has been set up in a garden shed. A tackle has been rigged to pull the head away to the right, thus stretching the luff and inducing a fold in the cloth; this is evidence of draft in the sail. The slightly uneven distribution of draft was cured by forcing one of the luff seizings back to its correct position.* Author.

else's boat, when his sail becomes narrow gutted aloft and yours joins the ranks of firm, round, bursting bosoms you have so long admired on your rivals.

Checks Ashore

Test Rig. Every owner of a light dinghy has his own shore test rig: head the boat 30 to 40 degrees from the wind and hoist the sails in the dinghy park. If you want to get close up to the head, roll the boat on her side and let gravity pull the sails into their natural shape; you will then be able to walk all round, trying the effect of taking in a seam here or putting in a dart there by pinching the cloth into a pleat.

Cruiser owners need not feel completely left out of it. All jibs can be set up horizontally by making fast the tack and then pulling out the luff by means of a tackle to a suitable tree – leverage is needed because the luff has to be nice and tight (your halyard will have some kind of purchase in the shape of a tackle or winch).

Leeches. A shore rig can often give confirmation of trouble spotted afloat. Set up a jib horizontally and get someone to pull the clew out to one side so that the sail shows its draft, then take a close look at the spot which has been giving trouble. You can often pluck the leech like a guitar string and feel the tabling taut under hand, so that it is obviously holding in the sailcloth. Conversely, the tabling may be slack to the touch, which tells you that it needs tightening. If the whole leech is flabby in to about 4 to 6 inches, then you need to tighten a seam or two. If the leech is tight for this distance, you have to ease the seams – but check further into the sail to see that there is not too much slackness well into the bunt of the sail. If there is, the cure may well be to *tighten* seams well in from the leech (which will have the effect of easing them at the leech itself relative to the rest of their length).

Experience is necessary when assessing how much to tighten or ease seams to cure leech faults. An average dinghy mainsail may only need two seams adjusted $\frac{1}{8}$ inch each, in to 6–8 inches. A mainsail for a 30-footer, on the other hand, may need two seams tightened by $\frac{1}{4}$ inch and two more by $\frac{3}{8}$ inch, over a

31. **Tightening a Mainsail Leech.** *Where the leech is slack, usually one seam is tightened between each pair of battens. The tightening is carried the full distance of the battens if the whole roach is slack, as in fig. 29 (a); where only the outer few inches are slack, as in fig. 29 (b), it continues for only 3 to 4 inches.*

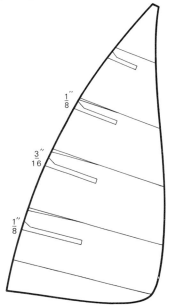

distance of 3 to 4 feet. All depends, of course, on the degree of slackness and how far it extends. You often need only tighten every second or third seam on a big mainsail, and you should always try to avoid adjusting those which come on batten pockets or which will require the racing number to be moved (fig. 31).

Draft. Setting up a headsail horizontally gives a wonderful chance to examine critically a sail which is seized permanently to a luff wire. This may be an old-fashioned way to make a jib, but there are plenty of them about, particularly on dinghies.

There are two main problems with the luff of a sail of this nature. First, the seizings round the luff wire may slide up or down the wire. When they were first put on, the luff of the sail was sewn to the tack eye and then pulled along the wire to be seized under stretch to the head eye, thus establishing the draft in the sail. This stretch, and thus the induced draft, was spread evenly all along the luff, whereupon seizings were put on at intervals, over the luff tabling and round the wire (I realise that many jibs with luff wires are left without these seizings, so that the wire is free to float inside the tabling, but we are examining the specific case where such seizings are present). If there has been movement, then the even rendering of the sail along the wire has been upset, and one part of the luff will have more induced draft in it than the other. This shows through a fold in the sail running only part of the way along the luff, to end in an ugly pocket. We shall see in the section on specific cures and remedies that the answer is simply to push the seizings back to their original place.

The second problem with a wire luff jib occurs when the draft has been semipermanently forced aft in the cloth by action of the wind (either because the sail is old and the wind has been blowing over it for a long time, or else it has been subjected to winds too strong for its designed performance bracket). Unlike a control luff jib, the luff is prestretched in the sail loft and permanently seized in place, so the draft cannot be pulled forward again by hauling harder on the halyard or Cunningham eye. If you suspect this problem, set up the sail horizontally, cut away all lashings round the luff wire – both seizings and hanks or snap hooks – then pull the luff by hand along the wire from the head or tack as hard as you can, while somebody else holds the clew out. If you cannot get enough purchase by hand alone, pass a thin line through the hank or snap eye which is nearest the head or tack, and haul on that. Watch the draft in the sail carefully and, if it improves, you will have to decide whether to return the sail to the professional for his attention, or to undertake fairly major surgery as described in the following chapter. Much will depend on the age and usefulness of the sail but, if it is old or blown out, it sounds as though you will not miss it much so my suggestion is that you have a go, even if only to increase your knowledge of sailmaking.

Sail Too Small. Nearly all mainsails and jibs look too small when lying slack on the lawn – or sail loft floor for that matter. As we saw in Chapter 3, most sails depend on being stretched for some of their draft, and this means that they need to start life rather shorter on the luff than their maximum size, so that they can be pulled out under action of halyard or outhaul (the exceptions are certain fully formed sails for some racing dinghies,

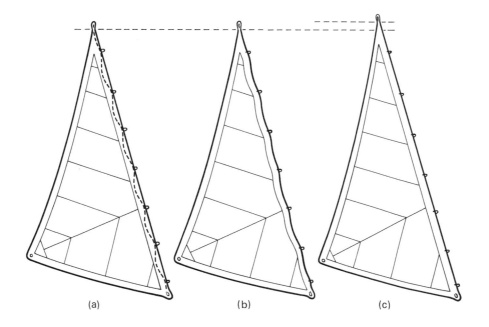

(a)   (b)   (c)

*32. **Jib Luff Measurement**. The luff of sail (a) is not pulled enough to stretch the cloth, and the luffwire is loose inside the tabling (except where it is seized by the hanks or snap hooks). The sail appears short, but the dotted line shows the wire. Sail (b) is similar, but the wire is sewn tight to the front of the tabling so it easily shows the kinks. Both these sails will look like (c) when they are pulled hard enough to straighten the wire and stretch the cloth fully, thus inducing draft in the luff.*

which are made of many tapered panels of fairly hard cloth). Even if a mainsail is made full length on the luff, the chances are that sewing on the luff tape will have caused it to pucker slightly; certainly this will occur where a rope is sewn directly to the sail, particularly if it is sewn by hand. A jib with a roped or taped luff will be similarly affected, while one with a wire seized at intervals to the luff of the sail will lie with the luff slightly twisted (as the longer wire waits to be pulled straight to stretch the shorter luff which is holding it in check), whereas one which is free to float inside the luff tabling will snake from side to side inside the tabling, again looking rather short (fig. 32). So set up sails on their own spars with a steel tape measure shackled on to the same halyard, then measure when they are under full tension. If a sail is, indeed too small, then it is a matter for the sailmaker, not only because the skills required are extensive (the sail has to be taken to pieces), but also because he presumably made it wrong in the first place so he should put it right for nothing (providing you gave him all the relevant information when you first ordered the sail). In these conditions you should preferably get the sailmaker to do his own measuring (he will be sure to check, if he is going to have to pay) but, if you are paying for the alteration and doing the measuring yourself, tell him the distance by which the sail is short of its marks rather than how long it is on the three sides. You might use different datum points from the sailmaker (aft face of the mast rather than the tack pin), or you might not pull it so hard as he will when measuring. There can be no doubt if, for instance, you ask for 6 inches to be added to the foot leaving the boom at the same height.

Sail Too Large. Once again, check actual distances on the spars. Reduction is easy for the sailmaker, but the lay of the cloth has to be consulted where the threadline angle at the leech is going to change by more than a couple of degrees or so (Chapter 1 shows how too much bias angle unsupported by tape or rope can result in slackness). A sailmaker would far rather be told to cut an exact amount off the foot than be asked to reduce the foot to stretched sizes of a certain distance, because once again he will not know exactly how hard you pull the sail on the boat, nor how much to allow for the tack fitting (which may or may not be a few inches aft of the mast).

Cross Measurements. If the oversize in question is one of not more than an inch on a cross measurement limited by class rules, and the sail is on the full side anyway, pleating the luff by this amount will make a quick and effective reduction without having to alter anything else. But before you rush into it, check carefully that you have taken the distance at the correct place. The half height measurement can be decided in at least three ways, resulting in three widely differing answers.

1. IYRU METHOD. The midpoint of the luff is found by folding the sail upon itself, with the highest point of the headboard nearest the luff even with the lowest edge of the boltrope nearest the tack. The midpoint of the leech is then found with the highest point of the headboard nearest the luff even with the lowest point of the sail directly under the middle of the clew cringle. The cross measurement is the distance between these two points, with the sail laid on the floor with just sufficient tension to remove wrinkles.

2. FOLDED LINE. The half-height cross measurement is taken along the line of the fold which is formed when the top forward corner of the headboard is placed on the bottom forward corner of the tack with the two halves of the luff coinciding and the sail smoothed out. Another way of describing this is to say that the distance is taken at right angles to the midpoint of the luff (though how do you take a right angle from a curved line?).

3. SPECIFIED POINTS. The cross measurement is taken between two points which are usually specified as being a certain distance down the luff and the leech from the head. This is open to misinterpretation on two counts: the sail may not be stretched enough when the datum points are marked, and the leech distance may be either on a straight line or else round the curve of the roach.

These are the most common methods, but there are others which may be unique to a particular class (for instance there is one which measures the half height from the midpoint of the leech – found by folding head to clew – to the *nearest point* on the luff). Finally, the rules may include or exclude the boltrope when taking the distance. So you can see that you have to be careful and know the rule for your particular sail, before you start laying into the sailmaker for inaccuracy.

eight
Correcting Faults in Set

We now come to the much more complicated sphere of fault correction. You should resist the temptation to get involved here until you have got some experience at sailmaking through carrying out your own repairs. Not only should you have a certain amount of dexterity with both sewing machine and with needle and palm, but you also need a good background knowledge of how and why a sail is made the way it is, so that you can assess the effects of any changes you may make.

Tightening Seams

To tighten a seam you have to mark the amount by which you wish to tighten it before it is unpicked. This may vary from $\frac{1}{8}$ inch to $\frac{1}{2}$ inch, but it will always taper off to zero where the seam runs on into the sail; only at the outer edge of the sail (usually foot or leech) will there be no need for this taper.

Having marked the run of the new overlap (the taper is to avoid the danger of a knuckle or crease appearing, so should not be too sharp), unpick the seam up to the point of the taper, put it under the sewing machine and sew to the new line. If you are dealing with a length of more than 12 inches, you should use double-sided sticky-back tape, or strike it up with match marks so there is no danger of one cloth creeping up on the next.

Where you are tightening a seam at the leech or foot, you must first of all unpick any tabling which may be fitted. If it is a 'rolled' tabling, integral with the sail and merely turned over, then you will simply tighten right out to the ends of the cloths. If it is a 'cut' tabling, that is to say one which has been cut off the sail and moved over to be replaced on top of the leech or foot so that the thread-lines continue to run in the same direction, it will be a separate narrow strip of cloth somewhere between 1 and 3 inches wide, possibly turned over at its edges to form a hem. Being cut from the sail itself, it will usually be made up of lengths of cloth sewn together – only where one panel runs the length of the foot or leech in question will the tabling be one length of material (except in cases where a special tape or webbing has been used). In any case, a cut tabling has to be shortened, or tightened, by the same amount as the seam itself.

Tightening Tablings

A diagnosis that the whole tabling has to be tightened will only be made where a cut tabling has been fitted. This is rarer than the reverse case (where the tabling needs to be eased), and means that the tabling has to be taken off from end to end, shortened very slightly, and put back again. In practice, it is easiest to start a few inches below the headboard and finish just above any reef cringle if fitted (to avoid reworking the latter) or above the leechline exit hole and tie-off holes (for the same reason). But you will need to lift the batten pocket ends, and the whole exercise is laborious and not particularly rewarding. My advice is to get a qualified sailmaker to check that this is indeed the trouble and then pay him to do it, even if you are dealing with the simpler case of a jib and not a mainsail.

Easing Seams

This, of course, is the reverse of tightening seams and the process is similar. You may find that the width of seam is marked on the sail, but the wise man will run a pencil down the lower of the two cloths before cutting the stitching. In this way there is no doubt about the original overlap, and the amount to be eased can be marked after the seam is opened up.

Easing Tablings

Once again, this is the reverse of tightening. It is more common than the latter, but it is no less troublesome and problematical, so my advice is once again the same: get a sailmaker to do the job for you.

Reducing Mainsail Roach

This is a major operation involving lifting the tabling and batten pockets, rerubbing the sail and then putting it all back again. It is, however, a fault correction which is likely to be correctly diagnosed and effective, and so is worth trying on a sail which is not your best racing mainsail.

The amount of roach you have to remove will dictate how far up and down the leech you must extend your attentions. Two or three inches at the halfway mark on a dinghy mainsail can usually be faired back to the old line of the leech somewhere near the quarter and three-quarter heights. If the sail has four battens, you should be able to leave the top and bottom pockets untouched and only have to lift the middle two; if there are three battens, you may be lucky and only have to lift the middle one – much depends on the amount of roach in the first place, even if you are only trimming off 2 or 3 inches, and you will not know until you have laid the sail on the floor and thrown a tape along the new leech. If you are having to reduce by 6 inches or more on a similar size sail, you will probably have to fair the new leech right to the head and clew. The same generalisation applies as proportions are increased on larger sails.

First spread the sail on the floor as described in Chapter 2. Stretch a twine from head to clew and measure off the amount of roach which already exists and check it against the batten length. It should not be more than one-third of the length of the longest batten, so decide on how much you want to remove and mark the point of the new leech on the sail. You should now throw a tape down the line of the new leech, taking due note of the conflicting requirements to fair the curve well up and down the sail, while at the same time not giving yourself more work than you have to, particularly where it concerns running into the batten pockets unnecessarily. Mark the sail in pencil for the full length of the new leech, which can be a straight line between batten pockets with advantage.

Remove completely those batten pockets which are affected, take off the tabling as far as necessary and then cut away the excess part of the sail, either allowing enough hem for a new rolled tabling, or trimming for the existing, separate, cut tabling to be put back. A cut tabling will be marginally too long for the slightly reduced periphery of the new roach, so you must measure carefully and shorten as required.

You now have to put everything back again, taking care to see that the leechline is properly installed. The batten pockets are refitted at their old levels, but extending further into the sail. The cure should now be effected.

Pleating

You will recall that this is the quick way to reduce round on the luff and foot of a sail, either to make it flatter or, in the case of certain mainsail clews, to draw off excess cloth which results in creases. In isolated cases, a luff pleat can also reduce a mainsail half height measurement by an inch or so, in order to bring it into rule.

A pleat can be as much as three inches on a large sail, but dinghies are more likely to be restricted to an inch or so, and this is what we shall consider here. Any sail which needs much more than this will be large and almost certainly made of 6-ounce material or more; three thicknesses of this would require an industrial sewing machine and is thus not suitable for home treatment.

A pleat must, of course, be tapered to nothing at each end so that there is no knuckle and the reduction of fullness is gradual. It must also not be too wide in proportion to its length, or else the sail will

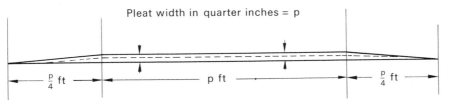

Pleat width in quarter inches = p

$\frac{p}{4}$ ft   p ft $\frac{p}{4}$ ft

33. **Pleat Formula.** *The full width of the pleat should continue at least over a distance equal in feet to the number of quarter inches of the pleat. The taper at each end should run for as near to a quarter of this distance as possible.*

be unevenly flattened. There is a broad formula which is useful for keeping within these two limitations. Turn the width of the pleat into quarter inches ($\frac{3}{4}$ in is 3, $1\frac{1}{4}$ in is 5, or 3 in is 12 quarters), and the full width pleat must then run up the luff for at least the same number of feet; it must also taper at each end for a quarter of this minimum distance in addition (but any extra length of the full width pleat does not require any extra length on the taper). In other words, a 1-inch pleat, which is four quarters, must run for a minimum distance of 4 feet up the luff and will have a taper of 1 foot at each end (fig. 33). In these calculations the width of a pleat is reckoned as the total amount of cloth to be taken out, which is twice the width of the final pleat when it is folded over on itself and sewn. Our 1-inch pleat will therefore show as being half an inch wide when sewn.

Assuming that you have decided on $\frac{3}{4}$ inch as being the amount to be taken out of the luff round of a dinghy mainsail, and that this should be taken from a length of some 4 feet (the minimum length being 3 ft for a pleat of this width) located around the one-third height point, spread the sail as suggested in Chapter 2. Mark off the 4 feet concerned within 2 or 3 inches of the luff, draw a straight line, and continue it up and down the sail for the required taper distance (9 in for this pleat, because a $\frac{3}{4}$-in pleat demands a minimum run of 3 ft, quarter of which is 9 in). Now draw another line $\frac{3}{4}$ inch nearer the luff rope and parallel to the first one, extending for the 4 feet in question; taper the ends the final 9 in, adjusting to a fair curve by eye. Fold the pleat on itself so that the two parallel lines are superimposed, and rub down to crease it in place. Finally, crease the taper to a point.

The problem is to start the work under the machine; the thicker the cloth, the more difficult it will be to make a neat beginning. As soon as the taper widens sufficiently, keep to the outside of the pleat and continue until you taper off at the far end; sew so that the zigzag stitching is alternately on and off the pleat. Cut off, turn the sail over and sew back along the other outside edge. Tie off the ends and the job is done.

If pleating the foot to reduce clew creases, you can afford to reduce the formula limitations by half, because draft here is not so critical of knuckles and, in any event, there will not be enough room for a long pleat and taper.

The beauty of pleating is that it is easy to undo again with no further damage than a few harmless stitch holes. Once you learn its secrets, however, it can radically alter the set of a sail with the minimum of effort. So easy is it in fact, that I cured a mainsail some time ago of a nasty fault by the simple process of putting in a short pleat. This was done by our service van at a regatta and the job took no more than 10 minutes, after I had looked at the sail set on its own mast. The owner did not deny that he had complained of the set for a long time and that his sail had been revolutionised, but he queried the amount of his bill for such a short job. I took hold of the invoice and reworded it as follows:

To: five feet of luff pleating	2.00
To: knowing where to put it	8.00
	10.00

He paid up without another murmur.

Too Flat

It is hard to make a mainsail any fuller without altering its size. If it is really too flat, in that pulling harder on the halyard or Cunningham hole fails to produce more draft up the luff, more canvas has to be found from somewhere to add to the luff round. As this cannot be conjured out of thin air, about the only way to do it without adding a new panel is to make the sail slightly smaller, so that the luff round can be relatively greater.

It is not, of course, quite as simple as that. Take the boltrope off the luff and spread the sail with prickers; stretch a twine down the luff to find the existing round. Fig. 34 shows how more round can be achieved by moving the headboard or tack.

Moving the Headboard. Take the board right out and unpick the tabling right down to the tack (which you should leave undisturbed), throw a tape to the new fuller line, adjusting as required to keep as long a luff as possible, and then pencil in the new luff. You now have to trim off the excess cloth and rub down to the new marks, either rolling the tabling or replacing the original cut tabling slightly shortened. Refit the headboard and patches, and rerope.

Moving the Tack. If you want to keep the

The effect of the former will be to shorten the luff and leech slightly, and bring the extra fullness fairly high in the sail. The latter shortens the foot and puts the fullness right down in the tack area. Both are lengthy tasks, with some risk to the set of the sail (largely from the reroping involved, at which the amateur may not be sufficiently practised to avoid uneven sewing and twists in the rope, unless it is sleeved in a tape), but either is worth trying on a sail which is otherwise no good to you.

Headsail. A headsail can nearly always be given extra fullness by putting more tension on the luff (see Pulling on the Wire below) or simply by easing the sheet. If extra luff round is really needed, the sail must be rerubbed as with a mainsail. This is best achieved by moving the tack eye aft, because fullness is needed low down in a jib. The wire has to come out for about half its length, and faired down to the new tack which should be an inch or so aft of the original. This will involve releasing the lashing at the head eye so that the cloth can lie slack in the process.

Clew Board

As I have said, creases from the clew are hard to remove, partly because they can stem from so many sources. One cure is to support the

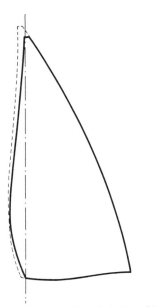

34. **Making a Mainsail Fuller**. *Only by making the sail smaller can it be made fuller without adding extra cloth. Either the headboard has to be taken aft down the leech, or else the tack has to be moved back to shorten the foot; or both.*

same luff length, take the rope off from a convenient point just below the headboard and carry it right round the tack eye; remove the tabling, tack eye and tack patches. Throw the tape as before, marking a new tack a few inches aft of the old one so that the new line of the luff forms a smooth curve, rub down and replace the tabling, tack patches and rope; work the new tack eye.

clew area by inserting a piece of stiff sailcloth or even plastic under the clew patch. If you are a racing man, the rules may have something to say about this, so check first that it is allowed; in any event, too large a clew board will make the sail unwieldy to stow or fold, so keep it reasonably small, say about the same number of inches across as the particular sailcloth weighs in ounces. You will find it impossible to fit one in a genoa which has tapes or webbing running radially into the sail from the clew ring; a clew board is thus really only practical on mainsails of dinghies and day sailers.

Undo the stitching round the inner end of the clew patch and under patches, until you have an envelope into which the board can be slipped. Cut a piece of 7–10-ounce sailcloth or thin plastic to fit, insert it into the pocket and sew down, through the board and over the ends. Don't use too much tension on any stitches which pass through the board, but see that it is firmly held in place.

Pulling on the Wire

When a headsail which is fitted with a permanently seized luff wire needs more tension on the cloth, it cannot be pulled harder by halyard or Cunningham hole, so it needs undoing and remaking. This operation is not so different from fitting a new luff wire as described in Chapter 5, but it is much quicker and easier.

Set up the jib horizontally as though examining for faults, and make sure that the luff is tight. If the seizings round the wire have slipped, so that the luff has moved over the wire and caused the draft to be unevenly distributed along the luff, with resulting pockets and hard spots, try forcing them back to their right place so that the tension is shared evenly along the whole sail. It can happen that this movement on the wire is caused by failure of the small eyelet in the luff tabling used for pulling the sail to induce draft up the luff (this will normally be hidden by a small casing at the head). The stress on the sail, coupled with the weakening effect of closely spaced stitches round the eyelet, can cause the cloth to tear so that the eyelet starts to pull out. The cure is to work a slightly larger eyelet in the undamaged cloth and, if you really want to reinforce a big sail, to fit webbing through this eyelet and down the sail for a few inches, along the lines of fig. 20.

If, however, the sail needs more tension all along the luff to draw the flow forward in the sail, cut away any seizings which go round the wire at intervals, but leave those on piston hanks or snap hooks if they look as though they are loose enough to allow the tabling to move along the wire. Take off any casing which may go round the wire between the head eye and the sail, and release the cord or twine which lashes the head of the sail to the head eye. The sail will now contract on the luff and slide back down the wire. With any luck the head eye will not be worked right into the sail in the same way as the tack eye, but will be formed on the wire which runs out at the head, so that there is an inch or so between the bottom of the eye and the top of the sail proper (fig. 18). If this is so, you merely have to shorten the head lashing, so that the sail is pulled harder on the wire, and then put back the casing and any seizings. If the sail is already pulled hard up to the head eye, you can pull until it just covers the eye, then lash it in place over the eye before cutting away some of the cloth and sewing it neatly down round the eye (fig. 35). This may mean doing away altogether with the small eyelet used for pulling the sail along the wire; in this case you may fit reinforcing webbing through the head thimble and run it down the leech for a few inches as an extra precaution. Though not essential, it is best if you can remove the thimble before doing this alteration and replace it afterwards to protect the new stitching.

Where both head and tack eyes are already worked in, you will need to shorten the luff of the sail by the appropriate amount. This will mean fairing off the leech as far as necessary, in a similar way to the reduction of

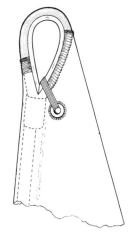

35. **Jib Eye.** *If the jib eye does not run well out at the head as in fig. 18, the sail can nevertheless be pulled to cover the eye if extra induced draft is needed. Some cloth will have to be cut away and the sail sewn carefully round the eye.*

mainsail roach which we discussed earlier in the chapter.

Reducing Spinnaker Fullness

If a spinnaker is too full in the head, some cloth must be removed. Fold the sail in two halves down the middle and spread it properly, doubled on the floor; conventionally this is done with the leeches to the left as you look at the sail from the foot, but this is not important. Pricker it out until it lies as flat as possible.

You now want to remove cloth from the arc of the upper middle fold, so that there is less fullness aloft. Throw a tape from the head eye and let it lie in a curve inside the curve of the sail, tapering back to the line of the middle fold at each end so that it does not start too sharply and also fairs smoothly into the sail somewhere near the half height position. You can either mark the sail with a pencil or, if it will not show pencil marks well, with a series of pricker holes (but try a ballpoint pen before you resort to this). Remove the tape and cut the sail with a hot soldering iron 1 inch outside this line, to allow for the joining seam.

Unpick the seam for 6 inches or so at the top and bottom of the cut, rub the sail down to the new line and then join together again, doubling the seam in the same manner as it was originally.

Spinnaker Leech Curl

Wires. Some larger spinnakers are still fitted with wires down the leeches for added strength. These can be a source of trouble, the two most likely faults being the breaking of one or both wires, and leech curl caused by too much tension. Removal of the wires altogether will almost certainly cure this, but you must be sure that the tapes are quite strong enough without them. On anything other than a large or a heavy-weather spinnaker, therefore, the first attempt at cure for leech curl could be to remove the wires altogether. But slack them both right off at the clews first and see what happens on a test sail. If the tapes are not man enough, you will need a few inches of extra length on each wire so that the leeches may be allowed to stretch a little more, providing any class rule is not exceeded. The exact distance can only be assessed by experience (usually 2–3 in), or you may add a foot or so to each wire without forming a new eye at the lower ends until you have been afloat and tried various tensions. Mark the required point and take the sail ashore to form the eye; make both wires the same length (and within the rule, if applicable).

Tapes. It is more likely that a spinnaker will be made without wires down the leeches. In this case, the problem discussed above becomes one of repairing the tape or easing it. If the leeches curl, you must take off the tapes along the affected part, cut them and add two inches or so to their length and then sew them back again (but remember to keep within the class rule; this may mean shortening the sail itself to match the existing tapes). You should strike up the tape and sail before you start taking out the stitching. When you have added the extra piece of tape, pull sail and tape out side by side and strike up again with a different marker – ballpoint instead of pencil – so that the extra length is shared evenly throughout the cloth. The first set of strike-up marks will make a check that you are slackening the original tension at a steady rate.

Roping

Roping is no black art, particularly if you put the rope on loose in a tape, as shown in Appendix B, but it does take a good deal of practice to rope a sail by hand from end to end. There are many pitfalls, some of which I have indicated in Appendix B. If you decide that you want to rerope your sail the hard way, my advice is to choose an old sail to do it on, and get plenty of practice first.

Oversewing. In certain cases of a mainsail being too long on the luff by one or two inches, you may reduce the length by oversewing the whole boltrope by hand. The action of sewing will make the rope gather and be less likely to stretch, so the result will be a sail 2 to 3 inches shorter, but one which is slightly puckered at the luff when not pulled hard, so that draft does not lie quite so far forward. The amount by which you reduce the length will vary with the tension you put on each stitch – pull them hard tight and you will gather the rope tighter. This is an excellent way of gaining practice in roping, because the rope is already attached to the sail, so you do not have to worry about match marks or twist.

nine

Alterations to Size

Major alterations to the size of a sail must change the relative position of any shaping which was built in when it was first made. There is therefore more than an outside risk that it will be spoiled for all time. Nevertheless, it is sometimes important to make these changes, and they can often be done successfully.

Naturally, there are limits to what can be done, depending on the original cut of the sail, and I am assuming conventionally laid cloths in this chapter. Even so, it is not possible to give a firm opinion as to whether a particular change can be made before you have had a chance to see the sail in question spread on the floor. There are sometimes snags which only reveal themselves when the twine is stretched round the sail to the new sizes, such as an awkwardly placed batten pocket, a row of reefing eyelets, or a window in the wrong place.

The most important single point to remember when deciding on a recut, is the bias of the cloth. We have been through all the reasons for containing the bias angle on the leech of most sails to within about 5 degrees, so I will not repeat them here.

Each requirement to alter the size of a sail therefore presents a different problem, and there are often many different ways of going about it. As a rule, small reductions in mainsails and headsails, and almost all reductions in spinnakers, are easy enough. The dinghy owner should remember, however, that there are some reductions which are too small: for instance it will not often be possible to reduce the foot length of a mainsail by much less than an inch, because anything smaller would cut through the middle of the original clew eye. Large reductions in mainsails or headsails may or may not be easy, and only a full examination of the individual case can tell. Almost all attempts to increase the size of a sail are complicated, and possibly not worth the trouble and effort, except increasing the length of spinnaker leeches.

Appendix C shows some of the detailed ways in which sails can safely be altered, and I have briefly summarised the attendant sail-making tasks. We shall now look at broad principles.

Reducing Mainsails

Let me illustrate the point about bias angle in a simple way. Assume that it is desired to reduce the mainsail in fig. 36 from a luff of 25 feet to one of 20 feet, leaving the foot as it is. If the head is dropped 5 feet, the measurements will be right, but the bias at the upper leech will be excessive and the leech will fall to leeward.

If, however, the sail is cut as shown in fig.

37, the leech will be undisturbed and should set properly in use. Agreed, we shall have to rerope the whole sail, and we shall be cutting away a good deal of the broad seam at the luff and foot – although some shape can be given to the new sail through luff and foot round. If we wanted to, we could add 3 or 4 inches to the length of the new luff, and then rip the seam at the new tack in to 2 or 3 feet, in order to taper the two sides of that seam by the 3 or 4 inches we had allowed. The headboard, racing number and all batten pockets

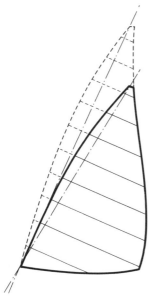

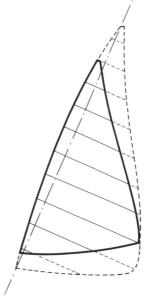

36. **Reducing a Mainsail** – 1. *Note how reduction of the sail to the dotted size puts the cloth on the bias at the leech.*

37. **Reducing a Mainsail** – 2. *By cutting the sail in at the luff, leech bias can be contained. The tack has been left on a seam so that broad seam can be built in if desired.*

would have to be repositioned whichever method were used (the headboard can sometimes be lifted complete with its patches and, indeed, the top cloth, to make things easier).

The above is not to say that a limited amount of extra bias cannot be accepted on a cut-down sail, particularly if it is going to be used for cruising or passagemaking. You can compensate for a certain degree of extra stretch by tightening the appropriate seams in the leech as described in Chapter 8, but you should be prepared for the worst.

Enlarging Mainsails

To enlarge a mainsail is a more difficult task. It is not a practical proposition to add a strip of cloth along the dimension which it is desired to increase, because conflicting bias will result. Moreover, due to the way the panels are laid, it is not possible to add to the foot length of a horizontally cut mainsail without putting a short length on to each panel all the way up the leech – not a feasible solution. This restricts us to the luff and leech, and these can be lengthened if the sail is split in two (usually at the tack seam) and a new panel added. The leech of the top part of the split sail will have to be faired into the line of the new leech, depending on how high

the luff is to go (rarely will this be exactly a panel width); alternatively, a part panel can be inserted to make the exact extra length required (see Appendix C).

Reducing Headsails

A good many of the foregoing remarks about reducing mainsails apply to headsails, with the added complication that many of the latter have mitres; horizontally cut jibs are somewhat easier. Any new clew should come on the mitre line, although there have been instances where it has been allowed to go above or below it with a fair degree of success. A new sail has the mitre in the clew for good reasons of stress, however, and I would not like to guarantee a sail where it started above or below that point.

A good method of deciding whether a certain headsail can be cut in a particular way is to draw it to scale and put in the mitre seam if it has one – this usually bisects the clew angle, but not always, so scale it off correctly. Next, use tracing paper to draw the reduced sail to the same scale, and then place it on top of the first drawing. You will soon see, by moving it about, whether you can get it to lie so that leech bias is within limits and so that the new clew comes on the existing mitre seam.

Plate 11. **Enlarging a Mainsail.** *A new strip of cloth being inserted in a mainsail at Gowen's loft, to make the sail longer on the luff and leech.* Hare.

If the sail can be cut in at the luff, without disturbing the clew at all, there will be every chance of success (fig. 38). Care should be observed with regard to the way the clew height will be raised or lowered by this method of cutting. In fig. 38 (*a*) the clew will be lower when set on the stay, while fig. 38 (*b*) will make it come higher.

38. **Reducing a Jib.** *Both (a) and (b) leave the important leech undisturbed; (a) reduces the foot alone, while (b) reduces both leech and luff. They both alter clew height.*

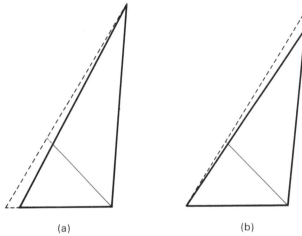

(a)   (b)

Enlarging Headsails

As with a mainsail, a headsail has to be ripped apart if it is to be made larger. This is major surgery, and usually all three dimensions, luff, leech and foot, will first have to be made bigger together, and the sail cut down again to the required new sizes.

To achieve anything like a reasonable sail, a seam should strike the luff at or near the point where the mitre meets it. Then new panels, or part panels, are inserted above and below the mitre to enlarge the sail; a horizontal jib only needs one panel inserted, usually just above the bottom panel. It should be noted that the result will be a sail with similar proportions to the old one. If it is desired to change any of these relative to the others, either the sail should be cut as we have already discussed, or else a mitre-cut sail can have this seam ripped and the clew angle changed as shown in detail in Appendix C.

Reducing Spinnakers

I am not concerned at the moment with alterations to the head of a spinnaker to make it flatter aloft, for we have already looked at this in Chapter 8. I now want to consider how a spinnaker can be reduced in maximum width or leech length, for instance to eliminate any penalty it may carry, or to convert a secondhand sail to a slightly smaller boat.

If it is made symmetrically, with a seam running vertically and many more running horizontally, a spinnaker offers a comparatively easy problem. To reduce the leech length, the first seam above the foot is ripped all along, the appropriate amount is cut from the sail and the wires or tapes shortened equally, and the two halves sewn together again. There is normally no broad seam in the lower half of a spinnaker of this nature, which is a simple rectangle, so there is no danger of disturbing the set of the sail. Doing the job this way means that the clews and foot do not have to be remade, thus making life easier (fig. 39).

To reduce a spinnaker in width, it is spread in half as usual, the racing number is lifted, and a slice is cut out of the middle. The vertical seam is then remade and the number put back. Once again the head and clews are undisturbed, but this time a certain amount of broad seam may be removed. Depending on how much narrower the sail has to be made, so will the reduction have to carry higher into the head where broad seam is involved (fig. 40). With a reasonable reduction in width, there is seldom any problem.

Enlarging Spinnakers

A similar approach can be made when enlarging spinnakers. It is easy to add a panel or

39. **Reducing Spinnaker Leeches.** *If the first horizontal seam above the foot is unpicked, a parallel piece can be taken out to shorten the height of the sail. Clews and head are undisturbed.*

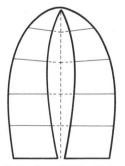

40. **Reducing Spinnaker Width.** *If the sail is split in two halves by unpicking the vertical seam down the middle, making it narrower is a question of trimming the right amount from the middle. The two halves are then joined together again as before.*

panels in order to make the sail longer in the leech. A horizontal seam is ripped as described above, and the new panel added to make the required length.

A thin tapering panel can also be added down the middle in order to make the sail wider. The result is neither aesthetically pleasing nor particularly good sailmaking, but it works very well for small increases, and is a good deal quicker (and easier) than fitting lots of short lengths to each panel; see Appendix C.

Spinnakers of Other Cuts

The above suggestions for reducing and enlarging spinnakers hold good for horizontally cut sails, with a vertical seam down the middle. Spinnakers can be seen nowadays, however, with panels laid like crazy paving, and these present different and difficult problems. The spherical cut, which has horizontal panels but no vertical seam, will allow small alterations to length of leeches, but any change in width will either entail manufacture of a seam down the middle, or else attention to the problem at both leeches; the latter means that the clews and wires or tapes will have to be remade, and possibly the head as well. On balance, if a sail of special cut has to be altered, it is probably best to put aside all

thoughts of keeping shaping, and to cut it boldly as though it were a horizontal sail. This will mean manufacturing extra seams across the line of the panels, and they will be unsightly and somewhat inefficient. It is surprising, however, what can be absorbed by the elastic nature of nylon, and this sort of alteration can often make a good cruising sail.

Altering a Mainsail from Slides to Grooves

A frequent modification is to alter a mainsail from slides to grooves. This entails rather more than might at first appear: the luff rope must be removed from around the top of the headboard and left with the bare end cut off at the top, so that it can be fed into the groove. In addition, the headboard will have to be reduced in size, so that there is a narrow space between the board and the luff rope; this is to allow room for the jaws of the groove. It is neither practical nor strong enough to add a small extra strip at this point (fig. 41).

Similar treatment will have to be given to the clew. It is a matter of luck whether there will be enough room between the existing clew eye and the rope, for the former to clear the upper edge of the boom groove (fig. 42).

The slide holes all have to be carefully

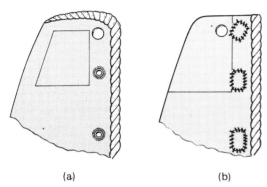

(a)   (b)

41. **Altering a Headboard from Slides to Grooves.**
*When a sail is fitted with slides as in (a), the luff rope is
usually carried round the top of the headboard, which
must be made narrower so that there will be room for the
sail to go inside the groove. The rope must be stopped at
the top, and the eyelets taken out and patched.*

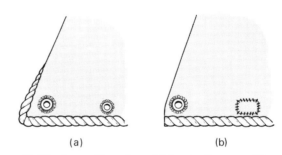

(a)   (b)

42. **Altering a Clew from Slides to Grooves.** *The
foot rope has to be stopped off at the leech, so that it can
feed into the groove. Patch the slide holes and pray that
there will be enough room for the groove between the eye
and the rope, so that you will not have to take out the
clew eye, patch the hole and then work another eye about
an inch higher in the sail.*

patched, taking care to see that the result is
not too bulky to run in the groove.

Altering a Mainsail from Grooves to Slides

The opposite of the last alteration is to alter a
mainsail from grooves to slides. A quick job
can be done by simply punching or working
eyelets along the luff and foot. This means
that an eyelet at the headboard will have to be
placed within the short distance between the

board and the rope (which used to run in the
groove), for it would be too far away from
the rope if it were placed through the board
itself (fig. 43).

The danger with this quick modification is
that the rope will pull away at the head, due
to the slightly weaker construction having to
withstand all the stresses localised at one
eyelet. If the sail were made for slides from
scratch, the rope would normally be taken a
short way round both headboard and clew eye
for added strength (fig. 41 (*a*)), but the
method is acceptable for most purposes.

The proper way to alter the sail is either to

Eyelets

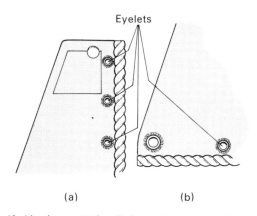

(a)   (b)

43. **Altering a Mainsail from Grooves to Slides**.
*Eyelets may be punched or worked into the sail close to
the rope, which will not run round the top of the headboard or clew eye, and will therefore always be marginally weak at these points; put two slides at the headboard to help spread the load.*

rub away a little cloth at the headboard, or to
fit a larger board, so that the rope is hard up
against it, thus allowing the slide seizing to
pass through the board itself as it should;
similar treatment is preferable at the clew.
However, a sail cast off by a modern boat
with grooved spars is often bought as a cheap
mainsail for an older sister with tracks on
mast and boom, and the method is a service-
able solution, providing the boat is not going
on a long passage where a rip at the headboard would prove embarrassing.

Appendix A
Sail Repair Equipment

The amateur sailmaker can spend a lot of money on a wide variety of gear, not all of which is essential for day to day work. As with most crafts, however, there is a certain minimum requirement which should form the basis of any kit (fig. 44). This appendix sets forth the full range of gear, not all of which is by any means essential.

Needles

Sailmakers' needles are triangular at the pointed end, with the body of the needle becoming round in section and narrower between the point or blade and the eye; the triangular blade makes a hole in the work large enough to allow a doubled thread of suitable size to pass. Most needles used for sailmaking are made of polished steel at Redditch in England, and they are not rust-proof so some sort of protection is useful. It is a good idea to wrap them in lightly oiled cloth and store in a tubular plastic bottle, such as a pill or hair shampoo container.

Sailmakers' needles are graded so that the round body of the needle conforms with the standard wire gauge, and sizes range from no. 6, which is over $\frac{1}{8}$ inch in diameter, to no. 19, which is as thin as a fairly stout domestic sewing needle; the size is usually stamped on one of the three faces of the triangular blade.

The professional sailmaker will tell you not to use too big a needle for fear of making holes in the sailcloth which are too large, and thus causing weakness and wrinkles; on the other hand, the larger the needle the easier it is to use. You are not going to remake a new racing sail but will more likely want to patch or resew a torn seam in an old jib, therefore speed and convenience should not be entirely subordinated to the need to avoid wrinkles – indeed the use of a more difficult small needle may cause the work to be poorer in quality than would have resulted from a larger and more convenient needle, thus in fact promoting wrinkles instead of reducing them. You should get by on most occasions if you have sizes 13, 16 and 18 available, plus a domestic needle for very light canvas such as spinnaker nylon. The table overleaf represents a fairly comprehensive kit for the man who likes to have it all.

When sewing three or four thicknesses of cloth, use a size larger needle with a heavier thread or four parts rather than two. When working on six or more thicknesses (head, tack or clew), go one heavier again.

There are many other types of needles, peculiar to special trades such as leather workers or upholsterers. These often have curved shapes which can be useful when sewing particularly heavy canvas which has to be tackled from one side, but the amateur sailmaker

Quantity	Size	Use
2	9	Whipping and seizing with heavy twine or thread
2	11	As above, on a smaller scale
2	13 or 14	Roping or working eyes on cruiser sails
2	15 or 16	Roping or working eyes on dinghy or trailerboat sails
6	16 or 17	Sewing sailcloth of 6–10 oz
6	17 or 18	Sewing sailcloth of 3–6 oz
2	19 or domestic	Sewing spinnaker nylon or light reaching sails up to $2\frac{1}{2}$ oz

need not seek them out, as his needs will usually be met by his own straight needles (but it is worth snapping up a curved needle if you happen to come across one).

Thread

The best thread for sewing synthetic cloth is Terylene or Dacron, and it comes in many weights and forms, which are graded in different ways by different makers.

Hand. Hand-seaming twine is usually prewaxed for convenience, and has a right-hand lay for the right-handed worker. The amateur needs a light twine (2 or 4 lb or a no. 1 or 2) for general sewing on dinghy sails and light headsails (3–4 oz cloth), and a medium weight (4 or 6 lb or a no. 3) for working canvas up to 6–8 ounces. The medium twine should also be used on dinghy sails and the like when sewing six or more thicknesses (head or clew patches) or for roping or working large eyes; for the same kind of attention to the heavier working sails, the medium twine may be used with four parts instead of the more usual two (but this will require a larger needle, which may make holes bigger than desirable), or else a heavy twine can be used. Use machine thread for any general hand sewing which has to be done on spinnakers and the like (eyes, however, should be worked with a light seaming twine).

Machine. Machine thread is usually left-hand lay and comes in a variety of plys and twists. The average domestic sewing machine will not cope with cloth much heavier than 3–4 ounces where more than two thicknesses have to be sewn, so the amateur will be restricted to a fairly light thread. Ask your

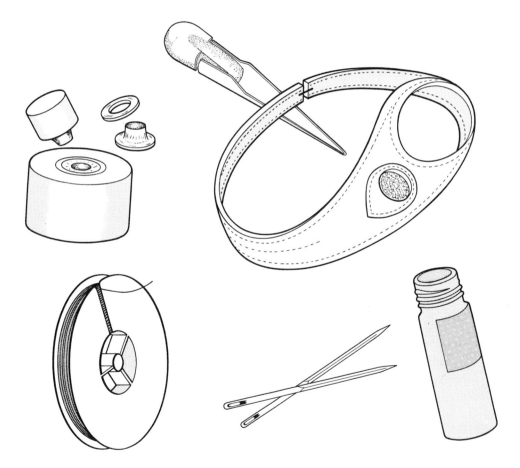

44. **Sailmaking Gear**. *Some of the more important items.*

sailmaker to sell you a spool for general purpose light use; this can also be used for hand-
sewing nylon.

Beeswax

Twine should be waxed before use to help
hold it together while sewing, and to act as a
protection; it often comes ready waxed on
small spools, and these are best. It is important, however, to have a small block of beeswax so that unwaxed thread may be treated,
and your sailmaker will probably be ready to
sell you one. If you don't have beeswax, a
candle will do in an emergency; even soap
will help hold the thread together while you
sew.

Sailmaker's Palm

It may be possible to push a needle through
light canvas with the aid of a thimble or by
bearing down on a hard surface, but this
quickly becomes hard work after any length
of time and, indeed, impossible with the
heavier weights of cloth. A palm is an important item, and you should get one and learn
to use it.

There are subtle differences between a
roping and a seaming palm. The former has a
large thumb protection to enable the twine to
be wrapped round it and pulled tight through
the rope, and its metal needle guard is deeper
set to allow for the greater length of the
larger roping needle. The seaming palm is
lighter and easier to use with shorter needles,
and is the one which the amateur should have.
There are *sailmakers'* and *sailors'* seaming
palms, the former being strong and the latter
lighter; both have a means of adjusting the
strap to suit the wearer, although this is
really superfluous. It is possible to obtain a
left-handed palm if you look hard enough.

Sewing Machine

Most sailors have access to a domestic sewing
machine, and this can make sewing a large
patch or strengthening a long seam into short
work. Professional sailmakers use a zigzag
stitch, in order to allow the cloth to stretch
and move, without risk of breaking the stitching; a machine with a swing needle is thus
the best, but straight stitch is acceptable if
nothing else is available. The longer the arm
of the machine, the easier it will be to handle
the sail under it.

The average domestic machine will handle
three or four thicknesses of cloth up to no
more than 3–4 ounces; you can double this
weight if you are merely repairing a seam of

only two thicknesses, particularly if the cloth is soft and with a fairly open weave. It is sometimes possible to buy a secondhand heavy duty tailor's model fairly cheap, perhaps foot operated (push pedal, not electricity!).

A sharp needle is required for penetrating the relatively coarse sailcloth, so see that you have one or two spares and can thus throw out anything which gets blunt (or breaks).

Fid or Spike

A large marlin spike, known as a fid to the professional, is often used when working eyes or cringles in a sail. It is used for reaming out the hole, and should have a maximum diameter at the large end of at least one inch, if not more.

Splicing Tools

Much synthetic rope is laid very tight, so that the strands are hard to keep separated during splicing. A special tool has been evolved to keep the strands apart and leave a groove down which the end being tucked can slide easily. An emergency alternative is to use a domestic crochet hook on the smaller ropes;

this is inserted from the opposite side of the strand, so that the end is pulled through.

Eyelet Punch and Die

If you are going to put in any eyelets, you must either sew round a ring properly by hand or else, if the strain on the eyelet is not going to be great, you may punch it in. This involves use of specialist gear in the nature of a punch and die, the thought of which may put you off. But cheap versions of these, together with a quantity of the appropriate sized brass eyelets and turnovers or liners, are sold in many stores dealing in tents and camping equipment. Their operation is usually explained on the back of the pack and they are easy to work (the Hipkiss eyelet kit is an example).

If you decide to hand sew a ring (reef eyes and Cunningham holes, for instance, should be hand sewn for strength), you will need the appropriate brass turnover or liner to fit into the ring as a protection for the stitching. This in turn will have to be fitted by the correct punch and die and, while your sailmaker may lend them to you if you are on good terms with him, he will be using them regularly and will not want to part with them for longer than overnight, so don't count on remaining on good terms; you are more likely to have to buy a set from the specialist supplier.

There is a circular cutter which forms part of the set for the professional, designed to cut a hole rather smaller than the ring in question; this is so that there shall be some cloth to turn up and sew round the lip of the ring. But we shall see elsewhere that this is not necessary, because a knife can do the job satisfactorily by means of cutting a small cross in the cloth.

Soldering Iron

A sharp electric soldering iron will cut and seal synthetic rope or cloth. If you are only going to get out your needle and palm once a year for a small darn or seam repair, then the hot iron is not essential, but if you are really going to undertake any serious repair work, I would strongly recommend buying one. It will save time and trouble in almost every job, but make sure that you get one which either has a knife edge or else is formed by bent wire no thicker than $\frac{1}{8}$ inch.

Seam Unpicker

There are tools with a hooked blade specially designed for slitting the stitching of seams.

Made of plastic with a small steel blade, they can often be bought in a store selling threads and ribbons. They are worth having as they are cheap, but they only work effectively on zig-zag stitching (Quickunpic is one example).

Bench Hook

A bench hook takes up little room and can help with hand sewing. The hook goes into one end of the work and is tied away to one side. One hand then tensions the cloth against the pull of the bench hook to steady the job, while the other does the sewing (fig. 46).

Adhesive Tape

I am not speaking here so much of sail repair tape, which is a first class item of gear to have aboard any boat, but of the more rubbery tape (which usually comes in red, blue or green) used to serve the ends of ropes or lines when they have been cut, or to tape over turnbuckles as antichafe measures; Lassotape and Sellotape are good examples.

There is also available a double-sided sticky back tape (in the Scotch tape range) which has revolutionised the problem of patching and seaming for both amateur and professional alike. It is used to hold the two

Plate 12. **Tools of the Trade**. *The palm on the left has a larger thumb guard and is for roping; the other one is a seaming palm and is best for all round use by the amateur.* Jarman.

cloths together while making a more permanent job by sewing.

Glue

At first glance glue may seem an unseamanlike item for a repair kit. But here again, it can do a good job of holding seams together or keeping a patch in place while a more permanent repair is made of it with the needle and palm. Clear Bostik is as good as any, for it holds well, is flexible and does not make a mess. Glue is not as quick acting or as clean, however, as double-sided sticky tape.

Leather

Leather in one form or another is often used as an antichafe measure, at clews in particular. You will usually be able to remove the old leather and use it again but, if it is badly torn or chafed, you will have to replace it. Ask your sailmaker to let you have a bit of hide (which is the raw skin and will be board hard until soaked in water for half an hour) or chrome hide, which is soft, treated leather, grey or almost green. A good substitute is a piece of really heavy sailcloth.

Sail Accessories

You will, of course, need from time to time the various accessories peculiar to your own sails: slides, hanks or snap hooks, wire, same weight cloth (it is worth asking for offcuts when you buy new sails) and window material. Any or all of these may be bought as the need arises, but the man who has a small stock will avoid having to wait until he can get to the chandlery, and may thus be able to get on with repairs which crop up at weekends.

Sundries

Serving mallets, stitch irons and the like are not necessary unless you intend shipping as sailmaker aboard a square rigger (in which case you will need more instruction and practice than you are likely to get from this book), but prickers or weights for holding a sail spread on the floor will be necessary if you want to be at all adventurous in your sailmaking. A sharp knife or a large pair of scissors is also essential, and a short ruler and pencil will often be found useful when patching. Finally, a piece of stout canvas spread over your knees will stop you sewing yourself to the sail as you work . . . and a bottle of Scotch will help in case you do.

Appendix B
Hand Work

Use of the Palm

The sewing palm should fit reasonably well with the thumb through the hole and the metal needle guard snugly in the middle of the palm of the hand (where else?). The beginner will be wise to stick a piece of adhesive plaster or tape over the back of the thumb just above the knuckle, because prolonged hand sewing can rub the skin raw. Hold the needle between the thumb and first finger so that the eye rests against the guard, then push the point into the cloth. As soon as it has entered, release your hold on the needle and use the palm of the hand to apply pressure to the eye by means of the guard. As the point comes out the other side, grip it with the finger and thumb again to help it out and pull on the thread. With practice this becomes almost one continuous movement, and it is worth trying your hand on an old piece of sailcloth for a while before you start in earnest.

Hand Twine

Having selected the correct twine, cut off about 4 feet; any less will mean frequent joins, and much more will make it unwieldy to pull through at each stitch. If the twine is not already waxed, draw a few inches of one

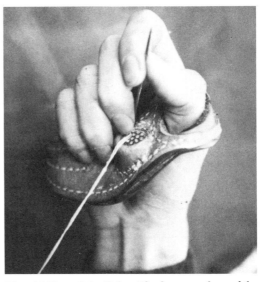

Plate 13. **Use of the Palm**. *The finger can be used for steadying the needle in position.* Jarman.

end over a beeswax block two or three times to make it hold together and easier to thread into the eye of the needle, then adjust so that the twine is hanging double. Now draw all of this doubled twine two or three times across the beeswax, so that it binds together nice and smoothly; if beeswax is not available, a candle makes a passable substitute, while soap will hold the twine together during sewing, even if it will not give a lasting protection to the stitches.

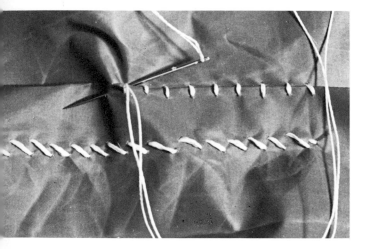

Plate 14. **Flat Seaming Stitch.** *The cloth overlap should be away from the worker and the needle pushed towards the left shoulder. The pattern of stitches is different on either side of the seam as shown.* Jarman.

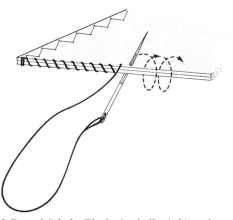

45. **Round Stitch.** *The basis of all stitching, the round stitch is used when you can conveniently get to both sides of the sail.*

Round Stitch

Modern sailcloth is so closely woven that hand sewing risks cutting the threads at each pass of the needle. Avoid spacing stitches too closely, therefore, and aim to achieve five or six stitches to the inch. For simplicity, start by knotting the twine (this will get you no marks from a trained sailmaker, who will sew the first few stitches over the unknotted end, but it will speed the job).

Most stitching is a variation of an over and over action, and the round stitch is probably its simplest form. If, for instance, the very edge of a sail has to be sewn, as when the foot of a headsail has chafed on the shrouds and caused the stitching to come loose on the tabling, the needle can go in one side and come out at the other. This involves pushing the needle through the edge of the sail, bringing it out on the other side and then carrying it round and back towards you, to push it through again in the same direction once more. It is best to sew from left to right, pushing up and away from you (fig. 45).

Tabling or Flat Seaming Stitch

Where a seam or patch has to be sewn in the middle of a sail, it will not be possible to push the needle through the work from side to side (unless there are two of you and you can pass it back and forth between you). This means that it must be pushed down through and then up again, all in one movement. The same stitch is used when sewing along the upper cloth of a tabling so as not to sew through a leechline.

Most people find it easiest to work from right to left, pushing the needle from the far side back towards their body (angled slightly towards the left) as it enters the canvas, but it can be done away from you. The needle should be entered into the sail close to the patch or tabling, and brought up evenly just

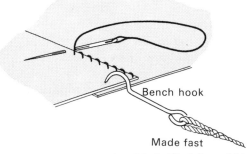

46. **Tabling or Flat Seaming Stitch.** *Work from right to left, and push the needle towards your left shoulder. A bench hook tied away to the right will steady the job.*

inside the edge of the second cloth, to be pulled tight before the stitch is repeated (fig. 46).

If you are sewing a flat seam, or indeed a large patch, there is a slight tendency for one cloth to slide across the surface of the other when sewing the first edge. It is wise, therefore, to hold the two firmly together by the use of pins, clear glue or double-sided sticky tape. After the first edge is sewn, the work is turned over so as to bring the new edge on top ready for the second row of stitching. Always sew a seam with the uppermost cloth nearer to you (unless you are pushing the needle away from you), so that the needle can enter the lower cloth first and come up through the upper cloth as it is pushed towards you.

Machine Sewing

Use of a sewing machine may not be exactly classified as hand work by a sailmaker, but you need your hands and, in any event, it falls naturally into this chapter.

A domestic machine will tackle cloth weights up to dinghy size, but beyond 3 or 4 ounces you should consider the heavier tailor's equipment; double this limit if you are only resewing a seam of two thicknesses. The kind of sewing you will be doing involves fairly long runs, so make sure that the machine is in good order and is well oiled; have a sharp needle and a spare on hand.

The heavier the cloth, the thicker the thread you should use and this requires a larger needle. With the needle lying on the table, the thread should lie comfortably in the groove of the body and draw through the eye easily when pulled by hand – but don't use a larger needle than you have to.

It is best to use a zigzag stitch because this allows the canvas to work without straining the thread, although a straight stitch is acceptable if nothing else offers. Regulate the stitch so that the link between the two threads comes in the middle of the cloth rather than to one side, and so that the two arms of each zigzag lie approximately at right angles to each other; this requires medium tension and a medium size stitch. The size of stitch may be increased where the cloth is heavy or where several thicknesses are involved. Try it out if possible on some off-cuts of the same thickness and weight as you propose sewing.

The standard claw feed on a domestic machine only operates on the lower of the two cloths being sewn together, and the slippery nature of synthetic material means that this lower cloth goes through the machine faster than the one on top, unless the operator holds it back with one hand and pushes the top cloth through with the other. If you are not using double-sided sticky tape, match marks put across the two cloths as they are 'struck up' while lying in place before sewing, help considerably in what has to be a continuing and conscious effort to keep one cloth from creeping up on the other.

When finishing off a row of machine stitching, leave 3 or 4 inches of thread free before cutting. Draw one of these ends through the work so they are both on the same side, and then tie them together. Cut off and tuck the ends between the layers of cloth with the help of a needle.

Roping

Rope in Tape. The easiest method of roping, which incidentally also allows adjustment, is to take a piece of tape 2–4 inches wide, crease it in half down the middle and lay the rope in this fold. Sew along the two parts of the tape as near to the rope as you can, in order to encase the rope completely, and then sew the tape to the luff of the sail, one fold going on each side. This obviates the need for any other form of luff tabling (fig. 47). The tape should be put on slack, that is to say so that there is more tape than sail, so pull the luff tight and ease the tape along as you sew. Even so, this method does not impart a great deal of induced draft unless the rope stretches easily, so you may need to allow for adjustment as follows. The rope must, of course, be made fast by hand sewing right through at head, tack and clew but, if you leave 2 or 3 inches sticking out of each end (at head and clew), you will be able to ease the rope should a trial sail prove that you need more stretch. So don't cut off until you are sure that you have got it right.

Taped Luff. If the sail is not particularly large, a tape can be put on the luff without any rope at all, in almost the same way; make sure you use a stout tape or webbing. It will have to have slides added, conventional ones for a track, or slug slides if the sail has to fit a grooved mast.

Hand Roping. Twists must be eliminated from the rope before it is sewn to a sail by hand, so that it lies evenly. Repair work usually involves putting a short length back on a sail, so it will probably already be attached for most of its length. If, however, a complete new rope has to be put on by hand, it should be carefully checked to see that it has no curls or kinks, and then held out taut while a pencil line is marked along it as a reference while sewing.

Rope has a tendency to shorten up during sewing so, if a specified length is to be sewn

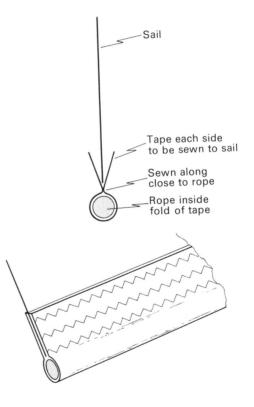

47. **Rope in Tape**. *The rope is free to move along the tape, apart from seizings at head, tack and clew. This is a simple method of roping for the amateur.*

48. **Roping**. *Practice is the keynote here, but only if you are proposing to put a completely new rope on a sail by hand. It is easy to resew a few inches which have pulled adrift. Blunt the point of your needle very slightly, to make it less liable to sew into the rope rather than between the strands.*

to a sail, it should be struck up at intervals of about 1 foot, in order that the length is shared evenly and the rope is not sewn on tight at any particular point. It is an interesting fact that most hand-sewn rope will lose some of its length during the sewing; an exception is some soft spun rope. If a sail has 25 feet of rope sewn to the luff and the rope is then taken off, it will be found to measure anything up to 6–9 inches shorter than when it went on. This is why a sail often cannot have its rope taken right off during adjustment, and then the same rope put back again – there would not be enough. If for some reason the same rope *has* to be used, it is best to use a fairly light thread and not pull the stitches too tight in order to reduce shrinkage. Conversely, if a sail has been roped slackly and stretches too easily on the spars, it can be made tighter by sewing over the rope a second time and pulling each stitch tight.

The actual process of roping can be fairly quickly assimilated as far as the beginner is concerned, for he will not normally be required to rope a sail from top to bottom, but rather to renew a short length which has pulled away. The finer craft of full-scale roping takes a good deal of time to learn, because consistency is important if wrinkles are not to appear from a ropebound sail. The edge of the sail should be towards you, over your

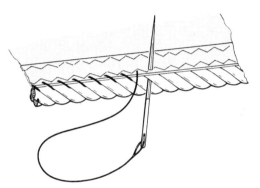

knees, and the rope laid just under the edge, which is turned up through 90 degrees for convenience of sewing. A bench hook, tied away to your right, is useful for controlling tension and steadying the job. Start at the left and, pushing away from you, pass the needle under one strand of the rope and then through the edge of the sail, in what is virtually the same movement as the round stitch. Pull the stitch tight and bring the needle back over the top towards you, and repeat the process under the next strand (fig. 48). It is important not to sew through a strand thus weakening it and causing irregularities in the lay of the rope, and it will make things easier if the point of the needle is dulled first, to stop it going too readily into the actual rope itself. It is also important to pull each stitch with the same tension and to keep taking the turns out of the rope as you sew.

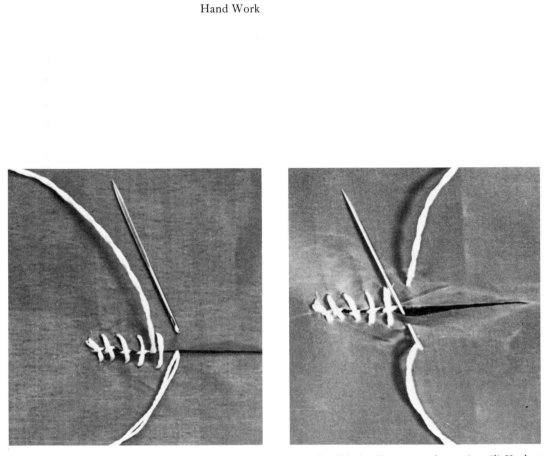

Plate 15. (a) **Sailmaker's Darn or Herringbone Stitch**. *This stitch will be familiar to many housewives. (b) Use just enough tension to draw the two edges of the tear together; too much will compress the cloth and cause wrinkles.* Jarman.

You will find that you have to make a conscious effort to use up all the sail before the next set of match marks is reached, and it is usual for the beginner to reach the mark on the rope before the one on the sail. Practise on a spare length for an hour or so before tackling any important job, and see that you advance the point of the needle slightly each time, after you have put it through the lay of the rope and before you enter it into the canvas.

Darning

Darning should be restricted to very small holes no bigger than the end of a cigarette, and should never be used where the canvas is known to be weak. Use a double, or even quadruple, twine of medium to heavy weight, with the smallest needle you can manage, so as not to weaken the cloth with large holes. Pass the needle under and over the first layer of stitching you put in, in the usual manner.

Sailmaker's Darn

This stitch is useful for gathering the two sides of a tear, either temporarily or as a permanent repair, and is the same as the domestic herringbone stitch. This is one of the few occasions when the professional sailmaker will knot the doubled twine at its end to form a stopper at the beginning of the work, which is sometimes rather looser than other sewing. Stitching is from left to right, and the start is made by pushing upwards through the far side of the tear. The needle is then brought back over the tear and passed down through the near side, to be brought up on the *left* side of the stitch thus formed (fig. 49).

After crossing over the top of this stitch, the process of sewing up through the far side is repeated. Each stitch should not be pulled tighter than is necessary to hold the two sides

*49. **Sailmaker's Darn**. You will doubtless recognise the domestic herringbone stitch. Don't pull too tight, but just enough to draw the tear nicely together.*

of the tear together. This is not to say that they should be slack, for their very job is to draw two pieces of canvas towards each other. To finish the job, the thread is usually tied off with a half hitch and tucked under.

Sailmaker's Whipping

An ordinary whipping will quickly come off the end of a rope or line in the normal wear and tear of working the boat, thus promoting frayed ends; the sailmaker's whipping is much more resistant. Thread a fine needle with light seaming twine so that two parts are put on at one time. Once again, most sailmakers will scorn to knot the end, preferring to leave a small tail exposed to be sewn over at the start to make an anchor; but you and I are not professionals, and we wish to know the simplest secure method, so we start with a knot – all the more so because it will be hidden between the lay of the rope.

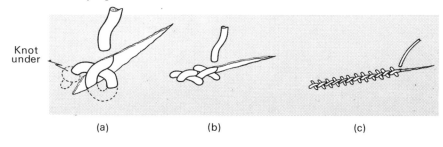

Knot
under

(a)   (b)   (c)

*50. **Sailmaker's Whipping**. The holding turns taken across the seizing are the vital ingredients here. Some authorities suggest doubling these turns, but this is a refinement which I would keep for big ship stuff, particularly as the thread should be doubled in the needle anyway.*

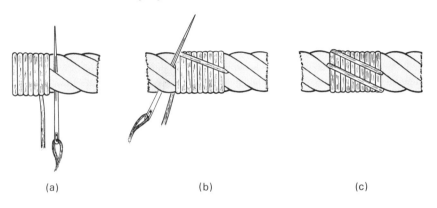

(a)   (b)   (c)

Wax the twine and sew through the rope so that a firm start can be made. Whip in the usual way, taking care to untwist the doubled twine so that the two parts lie evenly side by side and close up against the previous turn, then sew between the strands of the rope and out the other side. Lead the twine back over the whipping along the lay of the rope and sew again between the strands at the other end. Lead the twine back over the whipping, again along the lay, and repeat once more so that three passes have been made. Sew through the rope to finish off securely (fig. 50).

Repair Tape

I have included repair tape under hand work, because it represents a means of holding two parts of cloth together, just as a row of stitches does. It is stocked by most sailmakers and chandlers, and comes in a variety of shades so a multihued spinnaker need not be disfigured. The tape is self-adhesive, with a waxed paper backing which first has to be removed. It is about 2 inches wide and usually comes in rolls of 25 feet, so that quite long tears can be effectively mended. Designed primarily for emergency repairs to spinnakers, this tape will also work well on mainsails and jibs, and usually lasts so long that it tends to make the owner lazy. What should be a temporary stop-gap, put on until the sail can be properly repaired by needle and thread, becomes a permanent affair which is made to last for the rest of the season. There is not a great deal of harm in this, if it allows you to get more use out of your boat instead of sitting at home sewing.

There are also excellent adhesive-backed patches of various weights of Dacron sailcloth available to the trade in America. If these are trimmed to fit a small tear, they should be heat-sealed with a hot iron or knife to stop them fraying at the edges, but do not cut away any of the sail or you will be left with an exposed sticky surface; sew down all over the tear (this is therefore only a temporary job).

Insulating tape from the engine kit or adhesive plaster from the first-aid box both offer an emergency alternative.

Worked Eye

A hand-worked eye has two or three times the strength of one which is stamped in with a punch. If the eye is going to be subject to chafe on its inner surface (from a shackle or line perhaps), a brass liner or turnover should be clenched over the stitching with a punch and die as a protection.

First, the brass ring is laid at the desired place, and its inner and outer circumferences traced on the sail in pencil. Part of the inner circle is then cut out, either using a circular cutter rather smaller in diameter than the ring or, to avoid having to buy this special tool, by making two cuts with a sharp knife in the form of a cross; this allows some cloth to be turned up and sewn round the ring as it is put in. The brass ring is laid on the cut-out, and the needle passed down through the canvas outside the ring at any point on the outer circle marked in pencil, usually on the side away from the worker. The thread is pulled through downwards, leaving a tail to be sewn over by the first four or five stitches as a stopper (or knot the twine, if you like). The needle is then brought up through the cut-out and middle of the ring, passed over the top and down through the outer pencil line again, moving slightly round the circle each time. Ideally, a fid or tapered spike should be reamed through the partly worked eye at regular intervals during sewing, in order to keep the canvas spread and the stitches even. Each stitch should be pulled really tight, and a bench hook may be useful when working a large eye. The hook is tied away to the right and, after each stitch, the thread is laid across the left knee, which is used as a lever to pull away to the left and tension the stitch. Modern practice is to use four parts of thread, spacing the stitches rather wider apart than used to be customary, in order to reduce the risk of wrinkles.

When the circle is complete, the final stitch is pushed up and down a couple of times away from the ring and cut off. The liner is then punched into the sewn ring with the aid of the correct sized punch and die, to

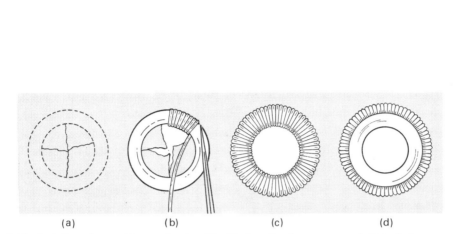

| (a) | (b) | (c) | (d) |

51. Hand Worked Eye. Learn this one, for it will add strength wherever you substitute it for a punched eye: Cunningham hole, slide eyelets, reef points, cover lashing points – they should all have hand worked eyes on a boat of any size.

protect the stitching against chafe of shackles etc, and the job is done (fig. 51). If several layers of cloth, for instance at the clew, make it hard to push the needle through, holes can be pre-punched with a pricker or small spike.

Punched Eyelet

If the eyelet is not going to have to support too much strain, for instance the snap hook or piston hank attachments on the luff of a small dinghy's jib, or the lashing points of a decorative cover, then it may be punched in.

There is one type of machine-fitted eye which has considerable strength. This consists of two metal rings which are pressed into the sail and held in place by a steel liner. If this gives way, it often takes some of the sail with it, and its replacement is one for the

sailmaker, unless you cut it away, put on a patch and hand work a new ring.

The most usual method on small sails, however, is to pass the tubular collar of a turnover or liner through a hole in the canvas, and then to spread the end of the collar over a flat circular eyelet; sometimes this circular eyelet has spur teeth to grip the cloth. The variety and size of eyelets is legion and each has its own correct sized punch and die; the system of identification is sufficiently complicated to baffle a computer, so I won't bother you with double O's, 3 B's, brassies, toothed grommets, liners, turnover rings or the like – go and pick out what you need from your local chandler.

It is particularly important when punching in an eyelet that enough canvas is available to be gripped between the two parts of the system. The hole should therefore either be made by pushing a spike through the sail, or else by means of two knife cuts in the form of a cross; neither of these two methods removes any cloth from the sail.

The turnover or liner is placed on the metal block, which will have a recess of the right size to allow it to sit snugly in place. The hole in the sail is forced down over the collar of the liner, the eyelet or ring is fitted over the liner and the pointed end of the punch is placed in the middle of this assembly. The initial blows of the hammer will force the collar of the liner to splay out over the eyelet or ring, and further hammering will cause the shoulders of the punch to squeeze the two parts firmly together. The correct strength to use will be learned with practice: too little and the parts do not grip together properly, too much and the turnover will be crushed and possibly split.

If you have the rings and turnovers but no punch and die, you can try spreading the turnover with a blunt spike or a centrepunch, and then hammering the two together using the ball end of a hammer – but try one or two on a spare bit of canvas first, because a lot can go wrong. For very small eyelets there is a single tool, rather like a pair of pliers, which does the job by squeezing the two sections together, but this does not normally exert enough pressure to make it particularly secure.

Cringle

It is sometimes necessary to work a cringle in a sail, either for an external tack eye or for a reef cringle. This is a rope loop attached to two small eyes on the edge of the sail (which themselves should be hand worked for strength), and it usually has a heavy gauge circular metal thimble wedged into it to protect it from chafe. It might be possible to punch in a large turnover and ring instead of the thimble, but a cringle often has to withstand considerable strain, so the machined thimble, with a bell mouth on each side, is to be preferred.

A single strand of a piece of rope should be unlaid, without disturbing the twist too much, to a length equal to about $3\frac{1}{2}$ times the circumference of the final cringle. The correct estimation of this length becomes important when a thimble of given size has to be forced into the finished cringle, and this only comes with experience. Put one end of the strand through one of the eyes and see that its ends are in the ratio of 2 : 1. These ends should be twisted together in the same lay and direction as the original rope. Offer up the thimble at this stage to see if it will fit. The cringle should look far too small, because it must eventually be stretched by force so that it can contract tightly round the thimble.

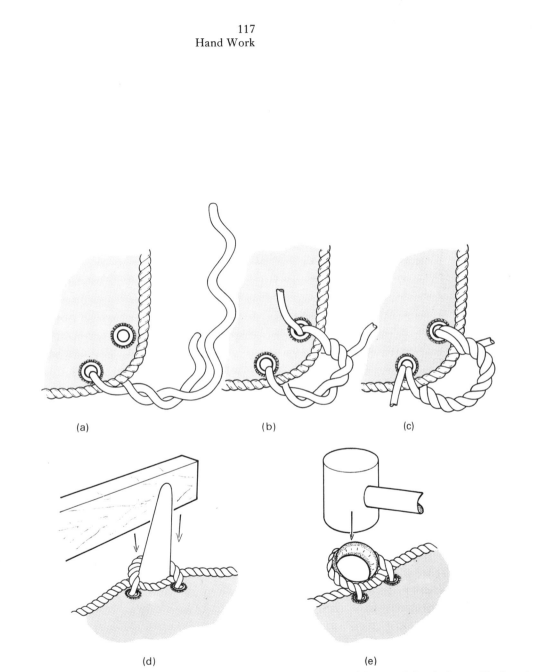

(a) (b) (c)

(d) (e)

52. **Cringle.** *You won't often need this one. Twist the two ends together in a ratio of 2:1, bring the long end back again to form a three strand rope; splice in the ends. The tricky bit is knocking in the thimble, but it's most satisfactory when you get it right.*

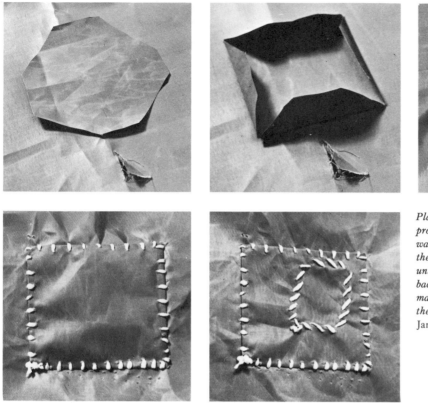

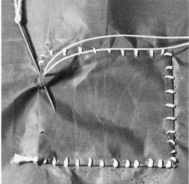

Plate 16. **Patching.** *The series shows the progress of a patch until at (d) the work was turned over. The stitches put in from the other side often produce the rather untidy result shown in (e) when turned back again (the mark of a competent sail-maker is to be just as neat both sides), but the patch would be quite secure enough.* Jarman.

The longer end is passed through the second eye and twisted back along the length of the partly formed cringle, to lie snugly in the twists of the lay and form a three strand rope once more. You should be careful to have enough of each end of the single strand left over at either end, to pass it through the eye and then to tuck it into the three strands of the cringle in the same way as a splice (fig. 52).

Try the thimble again for size; it should still look too big. Place the cringle over the tapered end of a large fid, with a piece of scrap canvas with a hole in it as protection on top, and hammer it hard down (ideally with a hide hammer) so that it stretches. You now take the cringle off the fid, quickly place the thimble on top with one lip tucked in and knock it smartly home with a hammer. The rope cringle will contract again on the thimble which, if the relative sizes have been correct, is now fixed for all time. If the fit is a good one, it will look as if the thimble will never go in, secondly you will have to be accurate when knocking it in and, finally, you will have to be quick or the cringle will contract before you have got the thimble home. If this happens, put it on the fid again and stretch it a bit further before having another try.

A Patch

If you can put on a patch without having to resort to self-adhesive materials or a heated soldering iron, you should be ready for anything, so let us examine the worst case first.

The tear should be pulled temporarily together with the herring-bone stitch or sticky tape, as this will make it easier to get the patch to lie evenly on the sail, particularly where the area to be covered is large. Draw a rectangle round the area it is proposed to patch, with its sides lined up with warp and weft if at all possible. Prepare the patch so that warp and weft are also lined up, and make sure that it is at least 2 inches bigger on all sides than the pencil marking on the sail,

to allow for a $\frac{1}{2}$-inch rolled hem (more, on large patches or heavy cloth). Cut off the corners of the patch on the angle, so that a half inch of cloth can be turned under to lie flat all round, rub this hem down to crease it in place. Lay the patch on the sail on the opposite side to your pencil outline, and fix it temporarily in place by means of pins, sticky tape or a few stitches. You next sew round the four sides of the patch using the tabling stitch, tackling the far side of the work and moving round as you go; put it on slack or it may tend to gather the sail into small puckers.

When you have sewn right round, turn the sail over, remove the temporary stitches or tape and trim the sail along the line of your pencil marks. Then cut into the corners for

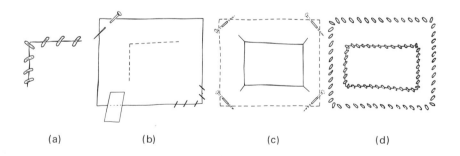

(a)   (b)   (c)   (d)

53. **Patch.** *If you fix the new cloth firmly over the tear before sewing, with warp and weft lined up correctly, creases can only be caused by putting it on too tight or by uneven sewing. Things became a lot easier when double-sided sticky tape appeared; and now self-adhesive patches are with us. There never were such times!*

half an inch, so that you can turn the hem under; rub it down to crease and hold it in place. Then table round this hem to complete the job (fig. 53).

Use of a soldering iron avoids the need for turning raw edges under, and leaves you with only two thicknesses of cloth to sew each time instead of three. You may still find it better to turn the edges of the trimmed sail, unless the tear is small and you can safely heat seal it first. If the tear is large, the new cloth will lie more evenly if trimming the sail is left until the patch has been sewn round once, but there is a grave danger of burning off both sail and patch if the iron is used too wildly at this stage. A self-adhesive patch makes short work of the job, but it should still be sewn. A particularly heavy patch can be made easier to sew by punching holes for the needle right through the work with a pricker or a heavy needle.

The quickest temporary patch job is to heat seal a piece of ordinary sailcloth and fix it in place by double-sided sticky tape, before sewing round to make a strong job of it; the tear is then sewn down as neatly as possible, without being trimmed, to stop it catching on obstructions. This will get you home, but do a proper repair later.

If a patch runs into a seam, this has to be unpicked first in the manner described in Chapter 5.

Splices

To prevent fraying, synthetic rope is best cut with a soldering iron. This will heat-seal the ends as it cuts, and the individual strands can be broken apart and unlaid for splicing; bind with adhesive tape to prevent unlaying too far. Touch up the ends with the iron again, taking the opportunity to taper them slightly to make them easier to tuck; alternatively, the ends may be sealed with a naked flame or whipped.

When using a soldering iron to cut off individual strands at the finish of a splice, keep the ends short and see that they melt and fuse with the strands of the rope. Take great care not to cut partly through any laid strand, or the whole splice will be weakened to the point of breaking. If you are cutting with a knife and then whipping the ends or sealing with a match, leave stub ends showing so that they do not work back through the strands. Roll or hammer the splice flat.

Use of a grooved splicing tool makes this work much easier; if you do not have anything else, a domestic crochet hook can be used if the rope is not too big.

Eye Splice. Tuck the middle end **a** against the lay into one strand at the appropriate point (plate 17a), and tuck **b** under the next

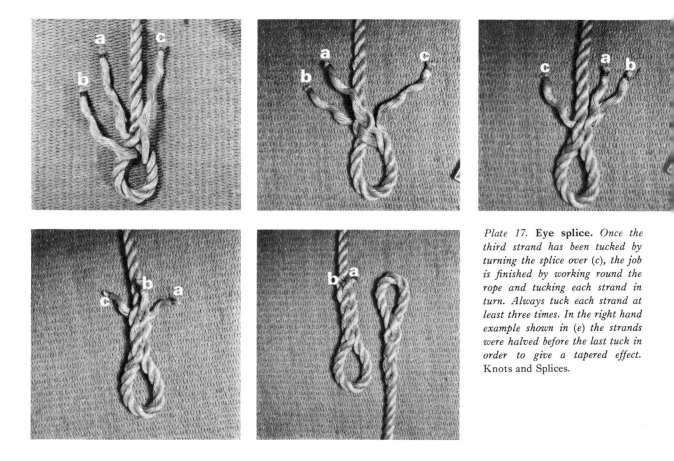

Plate 17. **Eye splice.** *Once the third strand has been tucked by turning the splice over (c), the job is finished by working round the rope and tucking each strand in turn. Always tuck each strand at least three times. In the right hand example shown in (e) the strands were halved before the last tuck in order to give a tapered effect.* Knots and Splices.

strand to **a** but nearer the eye (plate 17*b*). Turn the splice over and tuck **c** under the remaining strand in the same direction as the other two (plate 17*c*). Pull all three strands so that they are evenly placed along and round the rope, and then tuck each end twice more in rotation. Cut off and whip or seal (plates 17*d* and *e*).

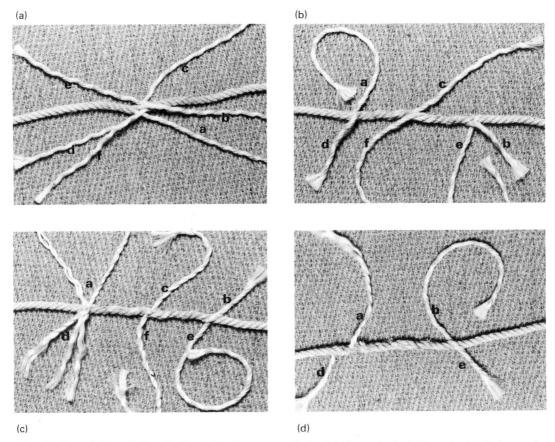

(a)

(b)

(c)

(d)

Plate 18. **Long Splice.** *If the splice is to be hand sewn to a sail, the finishing tucks should be made* with *the lay, so that the needle can pass easily between the strands.* Knots and Splices.

Long Splice. The long splice is weaker than the short splice, but it does not increase the diameter of the rope like the latter, and can thus still run in a mast or boom groove. Unlay the strands over a distance of about 1 foot, and engage all six alternately as in plate 18*a*. Unlay **a** a further 5–6 inches and lay **d** in the groove thus created. Do the same in the opposite direction with **b** and **e**, to produce the result shown in plate 18*b*. Divide each end in two and cut off one part of each division. Tie off the remaining pairs with a single overhand knot (**a/d**, **c/f** and **b/e** in plate 18*c*); tuck the tied ends into the rope (*with* the lay if the rope is to be hand sewn to the sail, or against it otherwise) two or three times over and under alternate strands (**a/d** in plate 18*d*). Cut off and seal all ends, both tucked and untucked, and the job is complete.

Appendix C
Altering Sail Sizes

It is easier to cut down the size of a sail than to increase it. Nevertheless, our examination of the effect of bias stretch shows us that great care has to be taken not to leave the leech, in particular, with the panels at too great an angle. A secondary factor to consider is the shaping which has been built in through broad seam and round; the cutting should remove as little of this as possible.

The following drawings show most of the more usual ways in which sails can be made smaller, and some of the more practicable ones in which they can be increased. I have assumed horizontally cut mainsails and spinnakers, and mitre cut headsails in every case, although horizontally cut jibs can be treated in a similar manner to mainsails.

Mainsails

Shorten Luff and Leech. There is a danger of upsetting the upper leech due to excessive bias at the head. Suggested safe maximum reduction is 5 per cent of the luff. Flow at luff and foot is undisturbed. Batten pockets and perhaps racing number may be disturbed. *Effort:* low. Headboard and pockets to move, leech to fair.

Shorten Luff and Leech. No disturbance to leech or flow. Amount of reduction dictated by resulting rise of boom as tack angle changes. Batten pockets may have to be repositioned to keep spacing even; also racing number possibly. *Effort:* medium. Headboard and pockets to move, luff to rerub and rerope.

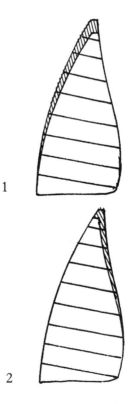

1

2

Shorten Luff Only. Disturbs broad seam at tack and foot. Clew will droop. *Effort:* low. Foot to rerope and new tack eye to work. Clew should not be disturbed.

Shorten Luff and Leech. Disturbs tack seam and foot seam. Foot is also very slightly shortened. Batten pockets may have to be repositioned to keep spacing even. *Effort:* low. As above, but new clew eye to work.

Shorten Luff, Leech and Foot. If strip to be taken off is nearly parallel, bias should be undisturbed, but there is always a danger when cutting a leech that its set will be spoiled. Shorter foot will alter batten length if I O R. All pockets must be moved anyway, so they can easily be shortened at the same time. Racing number may have to be moved. *Effort:* medium. Cut and rerub whole leech, move batten pockets, drop headboard, new clew eye.

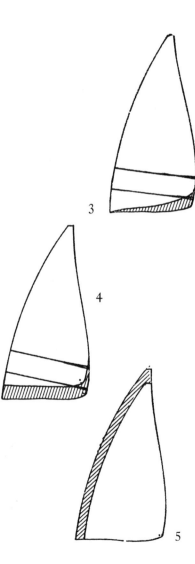

Shorten Luff, Leech and Foot. This is the best, and most protracted, method of reducing size drastically. Leech is undisturbed, but much broad seam is cut from luff and foot. Shorter foot may alter maximum permissible batten length and headboard size. Batten pockets may need repositioning to keep spacing even. Racing number may have to move. *Effort:* high. Drop headboard, rerub luff and foot and rerope, work new tack and clew eyes. Batten pockets and racing number as required.

Leech can be shortened further without shortening luff, by cutting up at clew.

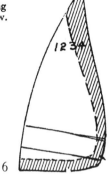

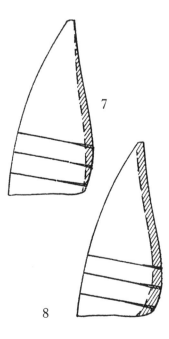

Shorten Foot. Cuts out much broad seam at luff. Boom will droop. Shorter foot may alter maximum batten length and headboard size. Should be able to leave headboard undisturbed if it is not now too big. *Effort:* low to medium. Take off rope, cut and rerub luff, new tack eye to work, rerope luff.

Shorten Luff, Leech and Foot. Cuts out much luff seam. Reduction may not result in same tack angle, so boom may rise or droop. Shorter foot may alter maximum permissible batten length and headboard size. Batten pockets may need repositioning to keep spacing even, and racing number may have to move. *Effort:* medium. Luff rope to come off, drop headboard, rerub luff, new tack eye, batten pockets to move, rerope.

Shorten Foot and Leech. Danger of upsetting lower leech due to excessive bias. Suggested safe maximum reduction is 5–10 per cent of foot length. Shorter foot may alter maximum permissible batten length and headboard size. Should be able to leave headboard undisturbed if it is not now too big. Lower batten pockets will move in, according to how high up the leech has to be faired. *Effort:* low. Cut and rerub leech, shift pockets, new clew eye.

Shorten Leech Only. No danger to leech or shape. Batten pockets may need repositioning to keep spacing even. *Effort:* low. Take rope off foot, cut and rerub foot, rerope. New clew eye, batten pockets as required.

Lengthen Luff. This is major surgery, and much depends on exact lay of panels and degree of lengthening. Sometimes 3 or 4 inches can be gained on the foot as well, by allowing the tack to go forward by this amount into the new cloth. Batten pockets will need repositioning, and reef points may be spoiled. *Effort:* high. Take off luff rope, rip tack seam, put in new panel, cut and rub new luff, rerope luff, new tack eye, drop headboard (this can often be moved complete with head patch and top panel), rub new leech.

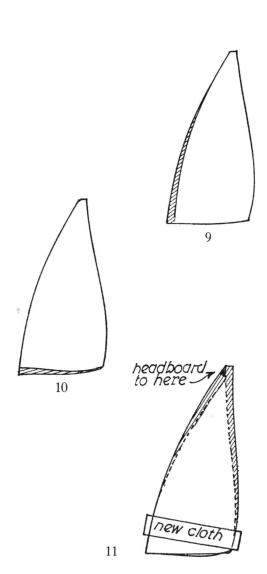

9

10

headboard
to here

new cloth

11

Headsails

Shorten Luff Only. Slight danger of upsetting the foot due to excessive bias. Clew will drop, as leech is not shortened, so sheet lead goes forward. *Effort:* low. Cut and rub new foot, shorten luff wire, work new tack eye.

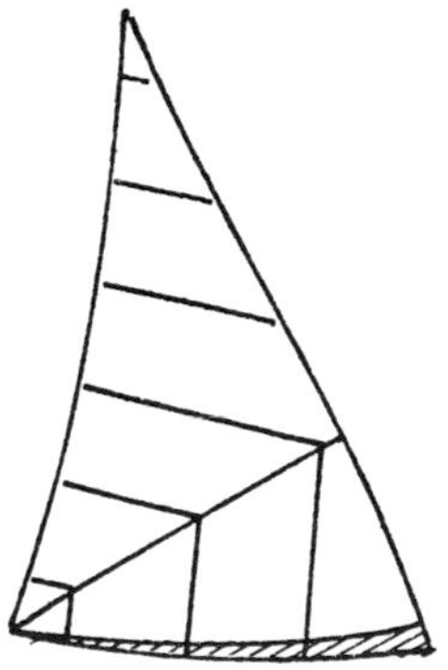

12

Shorten Luff and Leech. Danger of upsetting leech if too much is cut, due to excessive bias at head. Suggested safe maximum is 5 per cent of luff length. No other side effects from this cut, as the sheet lead stays the same. *Effort:* low. Cut and rub new leech, shorten luff wire, work new head eye.

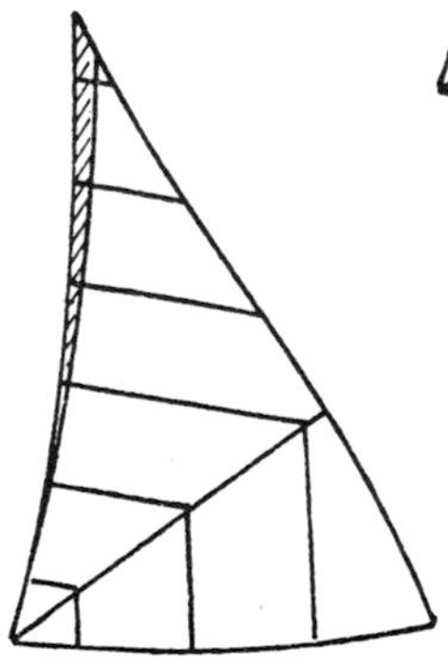

13

Shorten Luff and Leech. No danger to leech or foot. Clew will rise, and sheet lead goes aft. *Effort:* medium. Cut and rerub luff, take out, shorten and replace luff wire, work new head eye.

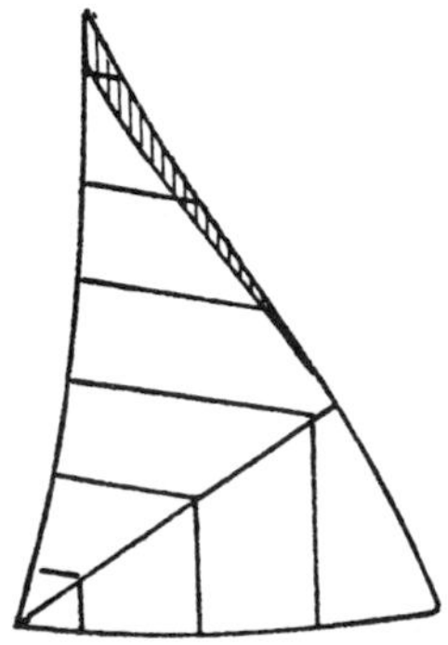

14

Shorten Luff, Leech and Foot. No danger to leech or foot. Clew and sheet lead will move according to whether strip cut off is a parallel piece or not. *Effort:* medium. Cut and rerub luff, take out, shorten and replace luff wire. Work new head and tack eyes.

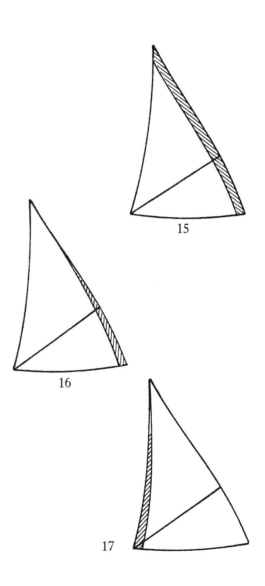

15

Shorten Foot Only. No danger to flow. Clew will drop so sheet lead will move forward. Depending on angle of the foot, so the luff may shorten slightly as well. *Effort:* low. Cut and rerub luff. Take out and shorten luff wire slightly (or let it run out at the tack), work new tack eye.

16

Shorten Foot Only. Danger of upsetting leech if too much is cut, due to excessive bias. Suggested safe maximum is 5 per cent of leech length. Clew comes off mitre: this is not a good method but can be done if clew not more than 5 per cent of foot from mitre, and it is then adequately reinforced. Sheet lead goes forward. *Effort:* low. Cut and rerub leech. Work new clew eye.

17

Shorten Leech Only. Slight danger of disturbing foot due to bias. Clew comes off mitre, see remarks immediately above. Sheet lead goes aft. *Effort:* low. Cut and rerub foot, work new clew eye.

Shorten Leech and Foot. Danger to leech and foot due to bias. Suggested maximum safe cut is 5 per cent of foot length up the mitre. Sheet lead stays the same. *Effort:* medium. Cut and rerub leech and foot, work new clew eye.

Enlarge Headsail. This again is major surgery. Usually all three dimensions, luff, leech and foot, will have to be made bigger together, and then the sail cut again to the required new sizes. This usually means a new luff wire, and the clew will move (and the sheet lead with it) according to the final size of the sail. *Effort:* high. Remove luff wire, rip two seams, insert two new panels (or part panels), rerub sail to new sizes, put in new luff wire, work head and tack eyes.

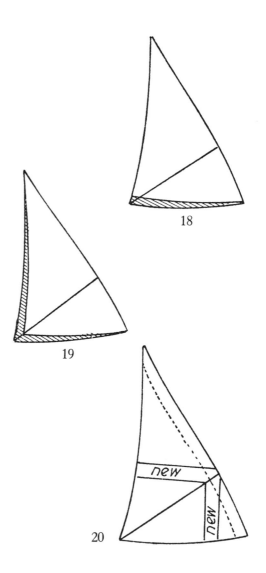

18

19

20

Headsail Clew Angle

The important point about cutting down a headsail into a smaller sail, besides bias angle, is the angle made by the clew. If this is the same as the original sail, the sail will cut by the luff to desired shape within its overall size.

It is sometimes desired to alter the angle at the clew of a particular headsail. This involves ripping the mitre seam, and then overlapping the two halves at one end or the other. The result is a shortening of at least two of the sides of the sail, which then has to have its luff rerubbed. The two illustrations at 22 and 23 are of the headsail at 21 above, with narrower and wider clew angles respectively. *Effort:* This sort of alteration is, in itself, a major job, but it is often combined with an enlargement of the sail along the lines of 20; this makes it a very lengthy modification indeed. It is usually confined professionally to headsails of at least 40 ft on the luff, because below this size it would be almost as cheap to have a new sail made from scratch.

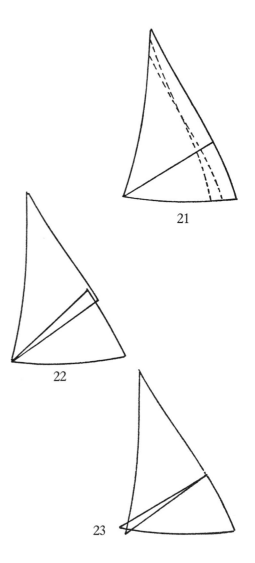

21

22

23

Flattening Mainsails and Headsails

Flattening sails is a common requirement and, as explained on page 71, an easy one. The sail is first set up for examination, and a decision taken as to how much luff round to remove. This is then done by pleating out the required amount, tapering away to nothing at either end. It has the advantage that it can be removed again by simply cutting the stitches to leave a double row of stitch holes which cause no harm. It is not easy to pleat less than $\frac{1}{2}$ inch, because this becomes $\frac{1}{4}$ inch on each side of the pleat, which must also taper to zero at either end. There is a minor risk of small creases radiating from the start and finish, where the pleat fades away to nothing. *Effort:* low. The examination of the sail takes the time here, and the decision on how much to pleat takes the skill.

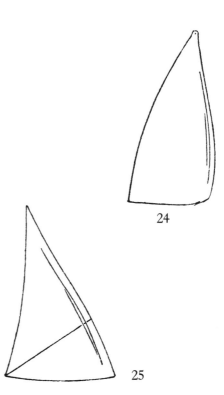

24

25

Making Mainsails and Headsails Fuller

It is not easy to make a sail fuller; the cloth is not there to provide the extra flow. It is not practicable to add a long strip up the luff, as this would set up counter stresses due to conflicting warp and weft. The best way to do the job is in combination with an alteration along the lines of figs 11 and 20 in this appendix, where the sail is taken apart and a new cloth inserted; this often gives the chance of increasing luff round in the process, but it is a lengthy business if no alteration in size is required. See also pages 82 and 83, if a slight reduction in size is acceptable.

Spinnakers

Make Narrower. A vertical section is cut from the centre of the sail; if necessary a seam has to be made (such as when cutting a spherical spinnaker in this way). *Effort:* low. Lift the racing number, cut the centre seam and remake it, replace the racing number.

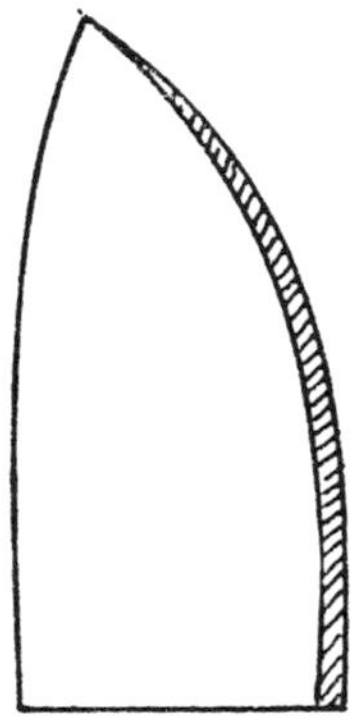

26

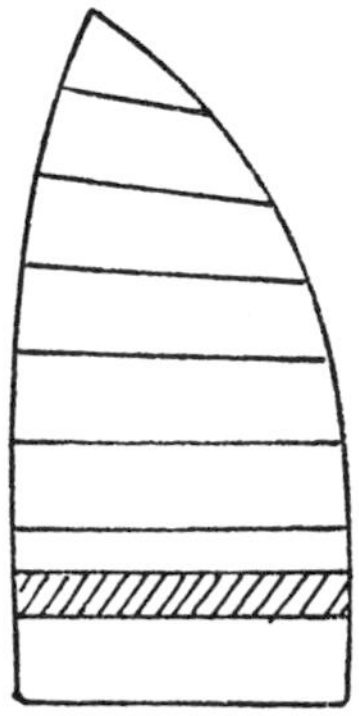

Make Shorter. A parallel piece is cut across the sail in the lower half, where there is normally no broad seam. Leave the foot and clews intact, so that the whole section can be sewn back to the shortened sail. *Effort:* low. Cut out the required section, shorten the wires or tapes, and rejoin sail.

27

Make Wider. It is possible, of course, to add a short length to each panel at the centre seam. This is, however, a lengthy business and no less likely to spoil the set of the altered sail because of the great amount of sewing involved. One vertical panel can be inserted in the middle of the sail with surprisingly good results. The shaping in the upper half of the sail will be disturbed, but the elastic nature of nylon seems to allow it to absorb the clash of bias angles which is inevitable. *Effort:* medium. Remove the racing number, rip the centre seam, insert a carefully tapered new panel down the middle, resew the racing number.

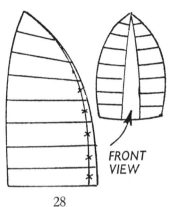

FRONT VIEW

28

Make Larger. This is a comparatively simple operation with no attendant dangers. It is virtually the reverse of the case where the sail is made shorter. *Effort:* medium. Rip a lower seam, insert a new panel of the correct width, splice or Talurit/Nicopress (with a double ferrule) an extra length of wire in the stays, or increase the length of the tapes if there is no wire.

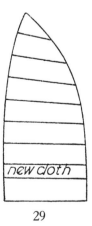

new cloth

29

Bibliography

Make Your Own Sails R M Bowker and S A
   Budd (MacMillan, London, 1957)
Racing Dinghy Sails Jeremy Howard-
   Williams (Adlard Coles Ltd 1974 and
   Quadrangle 1972)
Sailmaking Made Easy Bill Schmit (Water,
   Wind and Sail Publications 1974)
Sail Power Wallace Ross with Carl Chapman
   (Knopf 1975 and Adlard Coles Ltd 1975)
Sails Jeremy Howard-Williams (Adlard Coles
   Ltd 1976 and de Graff 1975)
Voiles et Grééments Pierre Gutelle (Editions
   Maritimes et d'Outre Mer 1968)
Working in Canvas P W Blandford (Brown,
   Son & Ferguson Ltd 1965)
Yacht Sails: their care and handling Ernest A
   Ratsey and W H de Fontaine (Norton
   1957)

Index

Figure numbers are denoted by italics

Acid, 26
Adhesive numbers, 27
Adhesive repair tape, 42
Alcohol, 29
Alkalis, 26, 29
Alterations
    angle of jib clew, 130
    changing from grooves to slides, 95–6, *43*
    changing from slides to grooves, 94–5, *41*, *42*
    enlarging
        headsails, 92, 129
        mainsails, 90–1
        spinnakers, 93–4, 133
    reducing
        headsails, 90–2, *38*, 127–9
        mainsails, 88–90, *36*, *37*, 124–6
        spinnakers, 92–3, *39*, *40*, 132
Ammonia, 27

Battens, 57
Batten pockets, 33, 39–41, *16*, *17*
Backwinding, 71
Badger slides, 53
Beeswax, 100, 105
Bench hook, 102, *46*, 110, 114
Bias stretch, 1–4, *2*, *8*, 10–11, 88–90, *36*, *37*
Biological soap powders, 27
Bleach, 28
Bloodstains, 27
Boltrope, 31–2
Boom vang, 60

Broad seam, 6–9, *7*
Brobat, 28

Carbon tetrachloride, 28
Casing, 32, 33, 45, 51, 52
Caustic soda, 27
Chafe, 20–1, 31–3, 35, 36, 43, 46
Chafing piece, 41–2
Chlorine, 28
Chloroform, 29
Cleaning, 24–9
Clorox, 28
Cloth construction, 1–2
Cloth weight, 4–5, *3*, *4*
Cover factor, 1
Creasing (*see also* Faults), 21–3, *12*, *13*, 29
Crimp, 1, *1*
Cringle, 116–18, *52*
Crochet hook, 101, 120
Cross measurements, 76–7
Cunningham hole, 11, 32, 50, 74, 84, 101

Dabitoff, 28
Darning, 111
Darts, 8, *7*
Detergents, 26, 27
Documentation, 62, *25*
Domestos, 28
Double-sided sticky tape, 55, 78, 108, 119–20, *53*
Draft, 2, 3, 6–12, *5*, *6*, *7*, *8*, 64, 72, 74, 82, 83
Drawstring. *See* Leechline
Drying sails, 24, *14*

Electrolysis, 52
Energine, 28
Examination for repairs, 31–5
Extensibility, 2
Eye or eyelet, 32, 33, 34, 35, *18*, 49–51, *35*, *43*,
    114–15, *51*

Faults
    creases
        clew, 66, *27*, 69–70, *30*, 83–4
        hanks, 67, *28*
        headboard, 26, 70
        leech, 68–70, *29*
        luff, 65–6, *28*, *30*
        rope or wire, 70
        slides, 66, *27*
        snap hooks, 67, *28*
    cross measurements, 76–7
    fullness
        too little, 71, 82–3, *34*, 131–2
        too much, 71, 131
        spinnakers, 85–6
    leeches 68–9, *29*, 73
        spinnakers curl, 86–7
    size
        too large, 76
        too small, 75–6, *32*
    spinnakers, 71–2, 85–7
Fid, 101, 114, *52*, 118
Fillers, 1–4, 21
Finishing process, 3
Flash, 28

Flat, sail too. *See* Faults
Flat seaming stitch, 36–7, 106–7, *46*
Folding sails, 21–3, *12*, *13*
Foot round, 6–7, *5*, 14–15, *9*
Forestay sag, 7, *6*
Full, sail too. *See* Faults

Genklene, 28
Glue, 103
Grease stains, 28

Headboard, 31, 45–6, *26*
Heat seal, 38, 42, 56–7, *23*
Herringbone stitch, 111–12, *49*, 119
Horizontal cut, 8, *7*, 90

Induced draft, *8*, 10, 84–5, *35*
Industrial smoke, 3, 23
Ironing, 29

Kicking strap, 60

Laminar flow, 59
Lay of the cloth or panels, 7, 12
Leather, 45, 104
Leechline, 32, 33, 39, 57–9, *24*
Leechline buttons, 58–9, *24*
Leech round, 79–80
Leech stretch, 19
Leech vibration, 29, 34, *29*
Luff hollow, 7, *6*
Luff round, 6–7, *5*, *6*, 14–15, *9*

Luff seizings, 74
Luff wire, 33, 46–8, *18*, *19*

Mast bend, 7, 69, *30*
Match marks, 42, 44, 45, 60, 78, 108
Metallic stains, 28
Methylated spirits, 29
Mildew, 3, 28
Mineral spirits, 29
Mitre cut, *7*, 91–2
Mr Clean, 27

Needles, 97–8
Nicopress, 43, 46
Notes, 62, *25*

Oiling plungers, 54
Oil stains, 28
Oversewing, 87

Paint stains, 29
Palm, *44*, 100, 103, 105
Palmit, 28
Patches, 41–3, 118–20, *53*
Photographs, 62, 64, 71
pH scale, 26
Piston hanks, 33, 53–5, 67
Pitch stains, 28–9
Pleat, 71, 80–2, *33*
Polyclens, 27
Porosity, 2
Powerpoint, 8

Prickers, 13–15, *9*, 82
Pulling on the wire, 83–5
Punch and die, 49, *99*, 101–2, 114–16
Punched eyelet, 115–16

Reefs, 32, 33, 50–1
Renuzit, 28
Repair tape, 42, 113–14
Resin fillers, 1–4, 21
Roach, 79–80
Rope, pre-stretched, 11, 44
Roping, 44–5, 87, 108–11, *47*, *48*
Round. *See* Luff round, Foot round etc.
Round stitch, 106, *45*
Rubbing down, 17–18, 43, 81

Sailcloth, 1–5, *1*, *2*, *3*, *4*
Sailcloth weights, 4–5, *3*, *4*
Sail covers, 23
Sailmaker's darn, 111–12, *49*, 119
Salts of lemon, 28
Sealed leech, 15
Seam chafe, 31, 33, 36
Seam, ease, 79
Seam repair, 36–8, *15*
Seam, tighten, 73, *31*, 78
Seam unpicker, 102
Setting up a jib, 72–4, 84
Sewing machine, 100–1
Shackles, 51–2
Shape control, 2
Size. *See* Faults

Slab reef, 32

Slides, 31, 51–2, *21*, 94–6, *41*, *42*, *43*

Smoothness (cloth), 2–3

Snap hooks, 33, 53–5, 67

Soap powder, 26, 27

Soldering iron, 38, 55–7, *23*, 102, 120

Spinnaker leech, 42, 86

Spirits of salt, 27

Splices, 120–2

Splicing tool, *44*, 101, 120

Spreading a sail, 12–15, *9*, 80, 82

Stability (cloth), 2–3

Stains. *See* Oil stains

Sticky tape, 55, 78, 108, 120

Stitches

    darning, 111

    flat seaming, 36–7, 106–7, *46*

    herringbone, 111–12, *49*, 119

    roping, 108–11, *48*

    round, 106, *45*

    sailmaker's darn, 111–12, *49*, 119

    tabling, 36–7, 106–7, *46*

Stitch unpicker, 102

Storing, 29–30

Stowing, 21–3, *12*, *13*

Streamers, 34, 60

Strike-up marks, 42, 44, 45, 60, 78, 108

Swarfega, 28

Swivel, 35

Tab hanks, 53, *22*

Tablings, 15–17, *10*, *11*, 38–9, 48

Tabling

    ease, 79

    tighten, 78–9

Tabling stitch, 36–7, 106–7, *46*

Talurit, 43, 46

Tape, repair, 42

Tape (in eye), 49–50, *20*

Tape (rope), 45, 108–9, *47*

Tape (slides), 51–2, *21*

Taped luff, 109, *47*

Tapering cloths or panels, 6–10,
    7

Tar stains, 28–9

Tell-tales, 34, 60

Tensile strength (cloth), 2–3

Tension on the cloth, *8*, 10–12

Test rig, 62–4, 72–4

Thawpit, 28

Thread

    hand, 98, 105–6

    machine, 98, 100, 107–8

Throwing a tape, *9*, 18

Turpentine, 29

Twine, seaming, 98, 105–6

Ultraviolet rays, 3, 23, 26, 36

Vang, 60

Varnish stains, 29

Velcro, 23

Warp, 1–4, *1*, *2*

Washing, 24, 27

Wax stains, 28

Weft, 1–4, *1*, *2*

Whipping, 112–13, *50*

White spirits, 29

Windows, 55–6, *23*

Wind tallies, 34, 60

Winter storing, 29–30

Wire, broken, 33, 43

Wire repair, 43

Zippers, 32, 53, 60–1